I0110645

THE BANANA TRAP

**How to Escape a Life of Stress and
Finally Break Free**

DR SCOTT ZARCINAS

OTHER BOOKS BY SCOTT ZARCINAS

Non-fiction

Your Natural State of Being
It's Up to You!

Fiction

Samantha Honeycomb
The Golden Chalice
DeVille's Contract
Ananda
Roadman

THE BANANA TRAP

**How to Escape a Life of Stress and
Finally Break Free**

DR SCOTT ZARCINAS

DoctorZed
Publishing

www.doctorzed.com

Copyright © Scott Zarcinas 2019

All rights reserved. No part of this book may be used or reproduced by
any means, graphic, electronic, or mechanical, including photocopying,
recording, taping or by any information storage retrieval system without
the written permission of the publisher except in the case of brief
quotations embodied in critical articles and reviews.

Copies of this book can be ordered via the author's website at
www.scottzarcinas.com, booksellers or by contacting:

DoctorZed Publishing
10 Vista Ave, Skye,
South Australia 5072
www.doctorzed.com

ISBN: 978-0-6485726-1-9 (hc)
ISBN: 978-0-6485726-0-2 (sc)
ISBN: 978-0-6487107-9-0 (e)

A CiP number is available at the National Library of Australia.

Because of the dynamic nature of the Internet, any web addresses or
links contained in this book may have changed since publication and
may no longer be valid. The views expressed in this work are solely those
of the author and do not necessarily reflect the views of the publisher,
and the publisher hereby disclaims any responsibility for them.

The author of this book does not dispense medical advice or prescribe
the use of any technique as a form of treatment for physical, emotional,
or medical problems without the advice of a physician, either directly
or indirectly. The intent of the author is only to offer information of
a general nature. In the event you use any of the information in this
book for yourself, which is your constitutional right, the author and the
publisher assume no responsibility for your actions.

Printed in Australia, UK and USA

DoctorZed Publishing rev. date: 05/10/2019

CONTENTS

With thanks to my wife, daughters, and extended family, without whom I would not have learned how to deal with stress...

WELCOME!

HELLO AND WELCOME. I'd like to congratulate you on taking this step to unlock the true potential of your life and embark on the process of de-stressing.

This guidebook is an alternative to quick-fix, result-driven recipes for 'success' in life. It is a process of knowing yourself better, a process of *how* to think, not a manual of what to think.

And because it is a process it is something that will continue throughout your life. There is no end to the process itself, which may seem contradictory to what the content of this book is about—de-stressing and living with greater joy and peace—but what you will find is that the process itself evokes the inherent joy and peace lying at the core of your being that has hitherto been suppressed and dampened by the stress of our modern lifestyles.

The process, therefore, means constant work on your behalf and to keep persisting with the process of stress management. As Martin Luther King said: "If not you, then who? If not now, then when?"

It is my hope and intent to now help empower you to the abundance and fullness that life has to offer using the specific knowledge of *The Banana Trap*.

Dr. Scott Zarcinas

A WORD OF ENCOURAGEMENT

THIS GUIDEBOOK IS not a magic wand that will make all your problems disappear. Nor is it a magic carpet that will take you to a place far from all your stresses and pains. On the contrary, this book will cause you to face up to your problems and urge you to resolve them.

But you are not without help.

This book will equip you with the necessary tools to master whatever stressful situation you encounter throughout your day.

As the parable says:

> *Give a man a fish,*
> *You feed him for a day.*
> *Teach a man how to fish,*
> *You feed him for a lifetime.*

THE BANANA TRAP

IN THE JUNGLES of Africa, legend tells of an ingenious method to catch chimpanzees called 'The Banana Trap'.

In a small cage, hunters secure a banana to one of its bars as bait. The cage itself is also fixed, usually to a branch of a tree, so that it cannot be wrenched loose.

Once set, there is only one way to access the banana: the chimpanzee must place its hand through an opening to grasp the bait. The chimpanzee is free to let go of the banana whenever it realises it's fixed and is just as free to remove its hand from the cage and flee to safety.

Yet the chimpanzee *will not* let go of the banana, even when the hunters have returned and are poised to bag their prey.

Herein lies the beauty of the banana trap: the chimpanzee has been trapped by nothing other than its own self—*it is a prisoner of its own desire.*

Seneca, a Roman poet around the time of Marcus Aurelius, said:

> *He who suffers before it is necessary, suffers more than is necessary.*

There is no need to suffer more than is necessary. For the rest of this guidebook, we will discuss how to escape the cage of stress and finally break free.

AN INTRODUCTION TO STRESS

'If you really want to escape the things that harass you, what you're needing is not to be in a different place but to be a different person.'

Seneca

HAVE YOU EVER felt overwhelmed and over-stressed? Is continual stress stopping you from doing what you want to do? Do you feel unable to cope with stressful situations?

Don't worry, everybody has moments of high stress and overwhelm! This guidebook is designed to help you understand why you experience stress, what you can do to break the cycle of chronic stress, and how to develop habits to de-stress and prosper.

When you can control stress, you can learn to feel less overwhelmed and more empowered and confident with what you are doing.

Stress, it must be said, is normal. But wouldn't it be wonderful to have $1 for every time you got stressed?

What's not normal, though, is to suffer stress every moment of the day for years and years. Unfortunately, this is the state of existence in which most human beings find themselves and its impact on individuals and the community is immense.

We live in an exciting age. We have at our disposal instant information at our fingertips. Technology has advanced more in the last 15 years than in the whole history of humanity. There are great benefits, but there is also a downside...

With the ever-increasing speed of technological advancement, we feel more overwhelmed and inundated than our parents or grandparents ever did.

Stress has soared by up to 30% in 30 years.[1] According to the World Health Organisation (WHO), mental health is associated with a significant burden of morbidity and disability. It also has a significant impact on world economies, with an estimated cost to the global economy of US$ 1 trillion per year in lost productivity.[2]

More so, mental stress claims are one of the most expensive types of workers' compensation claims in Western countries. Stress not only has the potential to cripple our own personal livelihood but also the potential to cripple business and national finances.

> Q: Given an average day, I would like you to rate
>   your underlying levels of stress as a percentage
>   from 0% to 100%.

This is the most important step of the whole process of de-stressing. So take your time, re-evaluate it if you need to, because your current level of stress will be the measuring stick with which you will monitor your improvement throughout this guidebook. Without knowing where you are now, you cannot plan where you want to be.

---

[1] Cohen et. al., Carnegie Mellon University, 2012.

[2] Including anxiety disorders and depression.

Q: In an ideal world, where would you prefer your
   stress levels to be?

For most of us, there is a big discrepancy between what
our stress levels are and what we would like them to be. Yet
although being totally stress-free might sound desirable, we
will discover that it isn't a realistic or entirely practical goal. In
fact, some stress is appropriate!

But if this guidebook could help you achieve an 80-90%
reduction in your current stress levels and *keep* them at that
'comfort zone' level, would you be interested?

Then let's begin...

PART I

THE STRESSFUL
BRAIN

1 STRESS DEFINED

'It's not stress that kills us, it's our reaction to it.'

Hans Selye

STRESS IS KNOWN as 'the silent killer' because of its correlation with the top six causes of death—cancer, pulmonary disease, heart disease, liver disease, accidents, and suicide.[3]

It has an effect on heart disease, high blood pressure, irregular heartbeat, and blood clots. The stress hormone, cortisol, also causes enlargement of fat cells and accumulation of abdominal fat, what's known as 'diseased fat'.[4]

Furthermore, stress is also believed to account for 30% of all infertility problems in both men and women. It kills brain cells[5] and is responsible for growth retardation in children.[6]

Interestingly, the term 'stress' wasn't commonly used until the 1930s. Until then, stress mainly described physiological, mechanical, physical, and biological forces, but it took an endocrinologist to popularise the word as we now know it today.

---

[3] *How Does Stress Affect Us?*, USA study, 2016.

[4] Lawrence Chilnick, *Heart Disease: An Essential Guide for the Newly Diagnosed*. Perseus, 2008.

[5] Gene Wallenstein, *Mind, Stress, and Emotion: The New Science of Mood*. Commonwealth Press, 2003.

[6] Bessel van der Kolk, et. al. *Traumatic Stress: The Effects of Overwhelming Experience on Mind, Body, and Society*. Guilford Press, 1996.

Dr Hans Selye is the author of *The Stress of Life*.[7] He studied the stress behaviour of rats and is famed for his work on the General Adaption Syndrome (GAS), which is a set of responses characterised by three phases: Alarm, Resistance, and Recovery/ Exhaustion. He asserted:

> *Every stress leaves an indelible scar, and the organism pays for its survival after a stressful situation by becoming a little older.*

Over eighty years on, however, stress has come to mean anything from a minor concern about what to wear to a party, to relationship difficulties, workplace deadlines, and global financial crises, so much so that the word has become a complex and multi-defined entity.

Words such as pressure, duress, strain, and catch phrases such as 'under the pump', 'high maintenance', 'up the creek', and 'in the doghouse', all refer to various levels of stress.

> Q: What are some of the words you associate with the term 'stress'?

The words you use are important because they not only reflect your understanding of what stress is, they are also a reflection of how you personally experience stress.

SUBJECTIVE STRESS

Like love, everyone has a unique, personal relationship with stress. What is stressful to some is a walk in the park for others.

---

[7] Hans Selye, *The Stress of Life*. McCraw-Hill, 1956.

Some seem to thrive in high-pressure environments, whereas others tend to wilt and fall apart.

Stress also depends on perspective. To an engineer, stress is some quantifiable mechanical force acting within a structure being built. To a parent, stress is a baby that won't stop screaming, even though all its needs have been attended to.

A look through the dictionary also reveals many various definitions of stress that encompass linguistics, mechanics, physiology, socio-economics, emotions, and situational events.

Stress is a noun, a verb, and an adjective. Furthermore, stress can be acute or chronic, short term or long term.

There is also 'good' stress, called *eustress*, which enhances function, such as strength training in the gymnasium. In contrast, there is also 'bad' stress, called *distress*, which leads to a deterioration in function or 'burnout' (see *Figure 1: The Human Function Curve*).

To encompass all the intricacies of 'stress', it has been defined by psychologists as: [8]

> *The psychological, physiological and behavioural response by an individual when they perceive a lack of equilibrium between the demands placed upon them and their ability to meet those demands, which, over a period of time, leads to ill-health.*

But before we can understand how to manage stress, we need to broaden our understanding of the origins of stress.

---

[8] Palmer, S. *Occupational stress.* The Health and Safety Practitioner, 7, (8), 16-18, 1989.

PHYSIOLOGICAL STRESS

Evolutionists explain the origins of stress on the instinct to survive. The 'fight or flight' response, as it is called, can literally save us, either by instigating a fight against the current threat to our lives or fleeing to a place of safety.

> Q: What recent experience(s) have you had of the
> 'fight or flight' response?

During the fight or flight response, hormones called adrenaline and cortisone flood our body, heightening our senses and reflexes in order to deal with the imminent threat.

Blood and oxygen are diverted away from non-essential organs—such as our stomach, gonads, liver, and pancreas—and re-routed to supply the parts of our body that will require extra sustenance—our heart, sensory organs, muscles, and brain.

Once the threat has been dealt with, however, adrenaline and cortisone return to normal levels and our body returns to its original, more passive state.

In the past where lions, tigers, and other predators roamed more freely than today, the fight or flight response meant the difference between eating dinner around the campfire with one's family or being the dinner itself.

In today's world, though, we are not likely to come face-to-face with a savage predator, yet we still experience threats to our personal safety.

Q: What are some events you might consider
   threatening?

At such moments you are experiencing precisely what your
ancestors did hundreds of thousands of years ago, even though
our world today is a much safer place to live.

Yet why do we still have stress? Is there anything we can do
about it? Is the complete absence of stress a realistic ambition,
or does it have at least some benefit?

THE HUMAN FUNCTION CURVE

Believe it or not, there is such a thing as 'good' stress. It is a
positive force, acting to improve our state of being and life-
situation.

As stated before, Dr. Hans Selye called this kind of stress
'eustress' in order to distinguish it from 'bad' stress, or what he
referred to as 'distress'.

Part of successful stress management, therefore, is the ability
to sift 'good' stress from 'bad'. It also requires some kind of
recognition that being totally 'stress free' is not necessarily a
desirable state of being.

Q: Think of some types of 'good' and 'bad' stress
   you have personally encountered and how they
   affected you differently?

Figure 1: The Human Function Curve graphs the relationship between stress (good and bad) and performance (physically and mentally).

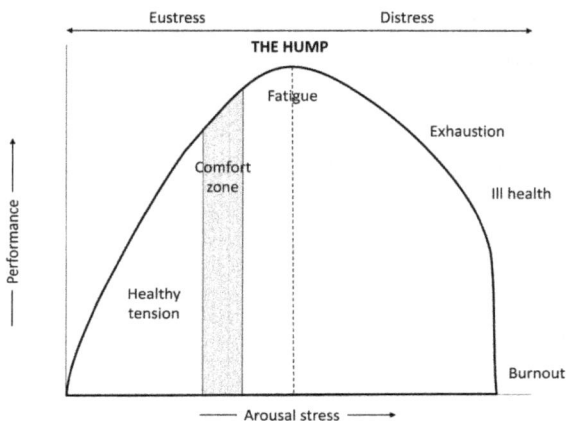

FIGURE 1:   The Human Function Curve[9]

One of the most interesting facets of this graph is that it is entirely personal. Although it represents the limits of the human organism in general, everybody has their own individual limits for stress. Furthermore:

Zero Stress = Zero Performance

In other words, to be 100% stress-free is to be dysfunctional!

The reason a little bit of stress is actually 'good' is because each of us has a degree of 'healthy tension' in which our body and mind function throughout the day. That's why it's important to understand which stress is appropriate for you and which is not.

[9] Adapted from Nixon, P: Practitioner, 1979.

Q: What instances of 'healthy' tension you are
   personally aware of?

At just the right amount of tension we also have a 'comfort
zone' in which performance is optimal, neither underworked
nor overworked.

AUTHOR'S NOTE:

Everything in this guidebook is designed to help you
achieve a 'Comfort Zone' of stress and *maintain* it
within that zone of optimum functionality.

Yet even if 'good' stress increases, functionality begins to falter.
Although an initial improved output or performance may occur,
the body and mind reach a 'hump' where fatigue sets in.

Q: Describe one or more instances where you have
   felt fatigued by too much stress?

With yet more stress, the body starts to lose coordination and
the mind loses concentration. We forget simple things. We
become easily irked and irritated. And if stress still continues to
be applied, exhaustion sets in and illness and disease begin to
manifest.

Q: What are some physical, emotional, or
   psychological symptoms of stress you have
   experienced, now or in the past?

Physical symptoms of stress may include angina, heartburn,

gastritis, anaemia, recurrent infections, general malaise, or weakness.

Emotional and psychological symptoms of stress may include excessive anxiety, insomnia, mood swings, and addiction.

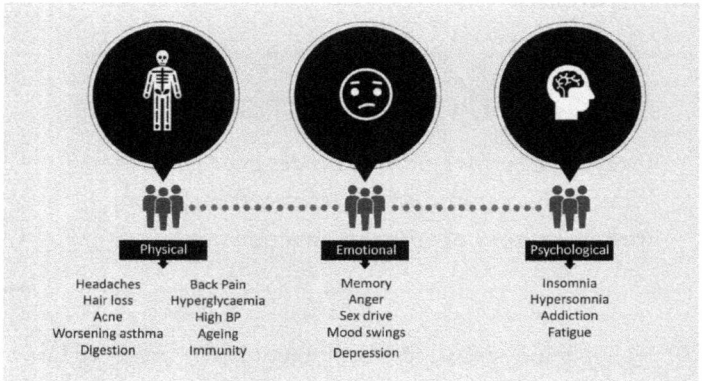

FIGURE 2:   Stress Symptoms

Finally, if stress becomes unrelenting, the body and mind break down completely. Angina may lead to a full cardiac arrest (heart attack). Gastritis may lead to ulceration and even perforation, with catastrophic haemorrhage (internal bleeding).

The mind too may breakdown to the point of complete dysfunction, with paranoia, overwhelming fear, psychological regression, and even, in its extreme, catatonia.

CHRONIC STRESS

Thankfully, however, stress usually isn't excessive and over-whelming. More often than not, it's something we learn to live with over an extended period of time.

Yet living in a constant state of stress, day in, day out, month after month, year after year, also takes its toll on our physical and mental health.

> Q: What effects of long-term stress have you
>   noticed in yourself or others?

Although adrenaline and cortisone have positive effects on the body in an immediately threatening situation, the body cannot cope in the long-term with elevated hormone levels.

It starts to breakdown, albeit gradually: arteries become clogged and friable; muscles melt away and atrophy; nerves become slow and hyporeflexic; bones become brittle and weak; vision blurs and hearing deafens; and chronic disease is not far around the corner.

In short, *chronic stress ages us.*

The mind, too, is greatly affected by chronic stress. Cocooned in a state of anxiety, either fighting the threat of danger or fleeing it, it also begins to break down.

Although breakdown may not be total and completely dysfunctional, as just discussed, the commonest states of a chronically stressed mind are: Dread, Despair, and Depression.

But do we have a choice? Or are we all destined to become helpless victims of stress?

Main Points:

1. Stress is the silent killer.
2. There is "good" stress, *eustress*, and "bad" stress, *distress.*
3. The origins of stress is linked to the "fight and flight" response.
4. There is a healthy "comfort zone" of stress for optimum performance.
5. Stress has physical, emotional, and psychological effects.
6. Chronic stress ages us.

2 STRESS: CONDITION & CAUSE

> 'Stress is caused by being "here" but wanting to be "there",
> or being in the present but wanting to be in the future. It's a
> split that tears you apart inside.'
>
> **Eckhart Tolle.**

As WELL AS being a physical, emotional, and psychological entity, stress is also a condition and a cause: it is a *state of being*, a condition, such as anxiety, as well as an *externally or internally applied pressure*, a cause, such as a looming deadline.

The dual nature of stress led Dr Hans Selye to split the definition of stress into two parts:

1. 'Stress'—the *condition* we experience.
2. 'Stressor'—that which causes or is a *stimulus* to the experience of stress.

According to the American Psychological Association *Stress in America Study* 2015, the leading causes of stress, or stressors, are:

1. Work.
2. Money.
3. Health.
4. Relationships.
5. Poor nutrition.
6. Media overload.
7. Sleep deprivation.

The Employee Insight Report conducted in Australia revealed that 68% of workers don't feel in control at work and that 54% of workers feel stressed at least weekly.[10]

At work, the most common causes of stress are: Workload (34%), Colleagues (16%), Poor work-life balance (15%), Job security (8%), Too much change (8%).

> Q: What are the main causes of stress, or 'stressors',
>   at home or at work for you?

As with stress, the causes of it have external and internal components.

> Q: Of the stressors you considered above, which
>   are external and which are internal?

The figure below highlights some common external stressors:

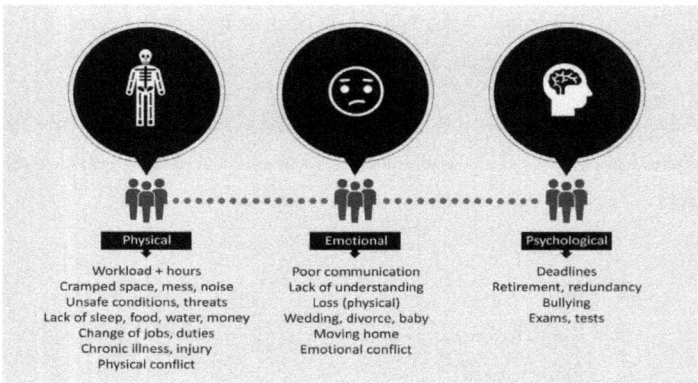

Physical	Emotional	Psychological
Workload + hours	Poor communication	Deadlines
Cramped space, mess, noise	Lack of understanding	Retirement, redundancy
Unsafe conditions, threats	Loss (physical)	Bullying
Lack of sleep, food, water, money	Wedding, divorce, baby	Exams, tests
Change of jobs, duties	Moving home	
Chronic illness, injury	Emotional conflict	
Physical conflict		

FIGURE 3:   External Stressors

---

[10] *The Employee Insight Report*, Sunsuper, 2018.

The next figure highlights some common internal stressors:

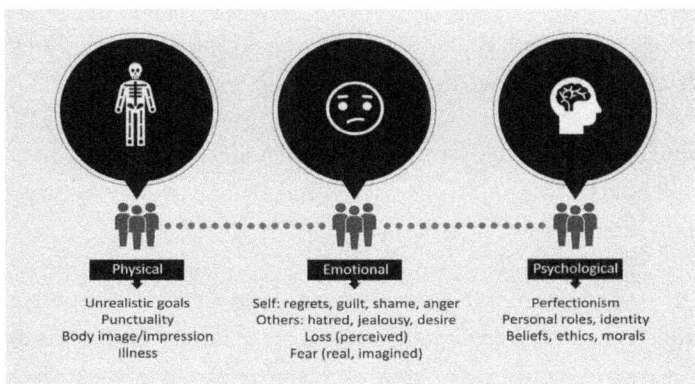

Physical	Emotional	Psychological
Unrealistic goals	Self: regrets, guilt, shame, anger	Perfectionism
Punctuality	Others: hatred, jealousy, desire	Personal roles, identity
Body image/impression	Loss (perceived)	Beliefs, ethics, morals
illness	Fear (real, imagined)	

FIGURE 4:   Internal Stressors

STRESS MANAGEMENT

Richard Carlson, the author of the bestselling book, *Don't Sweat the Small Stuff... and It's All Small Stuff*,[11] said:

> *Stress is nothing more than a socially acceptable form of mental illness.*

This may appear a little extreme, but what isn't extreme is the importance of stress management, which has been defined by the Gale Encyclopedia of Medicine as:

> *A set of techniques and programs intended to help people deal more effectively with stress in their lives by analysing the specific stressors and taking positive actions to minimize their effects.*

---

[11] Richard Carlson, *Don't Sweat the Small Stuff... and It's All Small Stuff: Simple Ways to Keep the Little Things from Taking Over Your Life.* Hyperion, 1997.

THE DEMAND-CONTROL MODEL

One of the best models with which to implement stress management techniques is the Demand-Control model, first developed by Karasek in 1979 as the 'Job Strain' model.

Since the 1990s, the Demand-Control model has been a popular tool used by psychologists to assess and analyse stress levels in an individual or team environment.

Given the impact of stress on businesses and national economies, the Demand-Control model is used especially by employers as a predictive tool in the workplace, but its use is by no means limited to there and can be extrapolated to suit any situation, personal or otherwise, in which stress is a significant factor.

The Demand-Control model involves several variables of demand and control, but we shall adapt it for our purposes and only use two: high demand and low control.

High Demand + Low Control = High Stress

Two possible avenues now open up for the management of stress, either in the workplace or personal circumstance: managing the *demand* placed upon you and the *control* you can exert.

Good stress management involves the management of both demand and control. But before we discuss stress management techniques that best align with the Demand-Control model, it's important to understand the barriers that prevent you from managing your stress.

THE 3 BARRIERS

Your brain is wired for survival, not for stress. Paul D. MacLean formulated the evolutionary model of the brain in the 1960s, which he called 'The Triune Theory of the Human Brain'.

This model divides the brain into three sections (*Figure 5: The Triune Brain*):

1. Neomammalian (Neocortex – forebrain)
2. Paleomammalian (Limbic – midbrain)
3. Reptilian (Cerebellar – hindbrain)

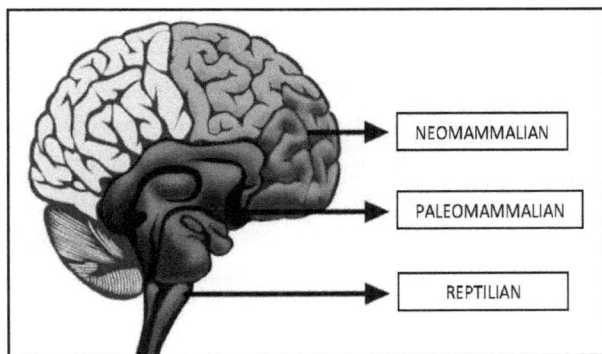

FIGURE 5:   The Triune Brain

Neomammalian means 'new' mammalian. It's the most evolved part of your brain and encompasses the area known as the neocortex ('new' cortex).

This forebrain is responsible for your superior human intelligence, which includes your thought processing, beliefs, reason, self-awareness, analysis, and planning. It is responsible for the conclusions you draw to external stimuli.

Paleomammalian means 'old' mammalian. It developed prior to the neomammalian part of the brain and is therefore less evolved. This midbrain encompasses your emotional processing area of the brain known as the limbic system, which includes the amygdala and hippocampus.

Its functions include your imagination, dreams, memory, reward, pleasure and pain. It is responsible for the emotions and feelings you associate with external stimuli.

The reptilian part of the brain is the oldest and therefore least evolved. This hindbrain is situated at the back of your brain at the top of the spinal cord, the area known as the cerebellum.

It is responsible for your most basic instincts, including breathing, heartrate, fight and flight, and your involuntary reflexes. It is responsible for the body's reaction to stimuli.

When navigating through the maze of stress to improved performance, productivity and wellbeing, there are therefore three main barriers standing in your way:

1. Instincts (hindbrain).
2. Emotions (midbrain).
3. Beliefs (forebrain).

Your reptilian hindbrain is wired to keep you alive at all costs. The first barrier to stress management is therefore your *survival instinct.*

Your paleomammalian midbrain is wired to react to any situation it encounters, and it usually does this through the dual filters of pleasure and pain. The second barrier to stress management is therefore your *emotional reactions*.

Your neomammalian brain is wired for reason and creativity. It perceives the world through the lens of your thoughts and imagination. The third barrier to stress management is therefore your *thoughts and beliefs*.

Each part of the brain acts like a filtering system, allowing only certain aspects of the outside world to filter through to your perception.

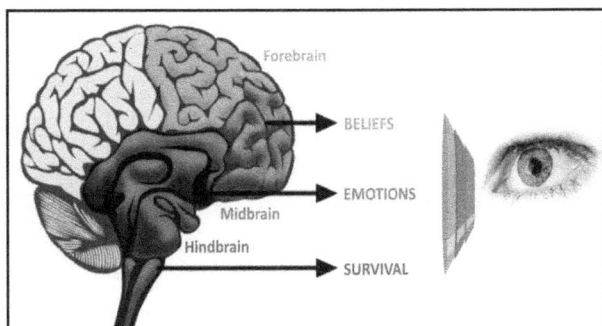

FIGURE 6:   Filters of the Brain—
Survival, Emotions, Beliefs

When your eye sees the outside, light stimuli pass through the eye's lens to the retina, where it then passes to the occipital cortex at the back of the brain via the optic nerve, where the stimuli is then converted into an image of what's 'outside'.

However, there is mounting evidence to show that there are more electrical stimuli passing from the back of the brain along the optic nerve to the eye than there is passing from the eye to the back of the brain.

This means you actually see what your brain is telling you it wants you to see. In other words:

You see what you believe.

As Gary Zukav, author of *The Seat of the Soul*, said:

What is behind your eyes... holds more power than what appears in front of them.[12]

What is behind your eyes—your survival instinct, your emotions, your thoughts and beliefs—is a two-edged sword: it can either work for you, or it can work against you.

Your triune brain can either help you overcome stress, or it can make your stress worse, because:

What you focus on you experience.

Your triune brain is powerful. But like electricity, which can either kill or provide life-giving energy, it must be tamed before it becomes a source of power.

Controlling your brain's reactions to stress is vital to your ability to manages stress.

---

[12] Gary Zukav, *The Seat of the Soul: An Inspiring Vision of Humanity's Spiritual Destiny*. Random House, 1991.

Main Points:

1. Stress is both the condition and the cause, both internal and external.
2. Stress management is a set of techniques and programs intended to help people deal more effectively with stress.
3. High Demand + Low Control = High Stress.
4. The Triune Model divides the brain into three parts—hindbrain, midbrain, forebrain—which act as filters to perception—survival, emotions, beliefs.
5. What you focus on you experience.

3 THE ABCD MODEL

'You can't always control what goes on outside. But you can always control what goes on inside.'

Wayne Dyer

ONE OF THE most stressful jobs in the world is the Emergency Physician. Emergency Room doctors and health workers need to be on high alert for any emergency to arrive. Heart attacks, strokes, motor vehicle accidents, poisonings, can arrive at any time during a shift, day or night.

Medical staff are drilled in emergency procedures. They are trained to perform under extreme pressure of life and death. But herein lies the key: they have been trained to deal with high stress.

As a medical doctor, I too was trained to deal with high stress events. When emergency situations arose, my training kicked into gear. I was so well drilled that I could almost run on autopilot. It was as though I knew what to do without thinking about it.

You too can take a leaf out of the emergency medical handbook and train yourself to deal with stressful circumstances at home, work, or other situations.

My ABCD model of short-term stress management is designed to help you do that. It is designed to help you bypass the three barriers of your brain that can prevent you from dealing with stressful events, so that you can focus and make clear decisions when stress arises.

This is the ABCD model:

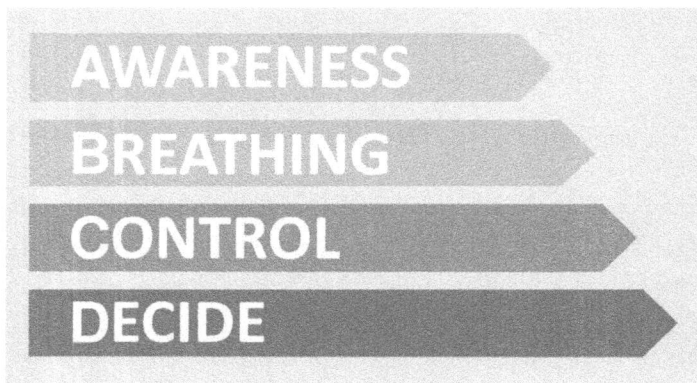

FIGURE 7: The ABCD Model

We will now discuss each of the four parts of the ABCD model in turn.

A: AWARENESS

In regard to the Demand-Control techniques involved for short-term stress management, awareness is the first step. Awareness negotiates the first barrier to stress-management—your reptilian brain and its survival instinct.

If you are not aware of how your triune brain is triggering your stress, your attempts to manage stress will be disjointed and limited.

Likewise, if you are not aware of how best to control your instinctive reactions to stress, you cannot respond with any degree of clarity and precision.

The first step is therefore to be conscious of the *internal and external demands* triggering your 'fight and flight' stress reaction and the physical, emotional, and psychological symptoms of your stress reaction.

Demand either comes from within or without, and there are two basic types:

1. <u>Internal</u>: the demand we put on ourselves.
2. <u>External</u>: the demand others put on us.

Internal Demand

The first type of demand, your own, is probably the easiest to deal with in terms of lowering your stress levels because it is the thing you have most power and control over.

> Q: What are some of the demands you put on yourself?

Look closely at those inner demands and consider whether there is a link between them and any stress you feel.

Figure 4: Internal Stressors lists common inner demands we place on ourselves, such as perfectionism, deadlines, personal image and roles, personal goals, right and wrong, as well as victim statements such as, "Couldn't. Shouldn't. Can't," and "Why ME?!"

Try not to make a judgement on these inner demands and label them as 'good' or 'bad', just observe whether or not they reflect and contribute to your own stress levels. Especially watch the words you use—"Couldn't. Shouldn't. Can't. Why me?"—as they have a significant influence on your stress levels.

Consider the internal demand of perfectionism. Being hard on yourself or putting yourself down over a mistake you've made or something you've said, or a standard you've failed to meet, can work two ways, much like 'good' and 'bad' stress:

- Positively: it can spur you to greater achievement and surpass personal goals.
- Negatively: it can mire you in apathy and failure.

But even if it works positively, the risk of too much perfectionism can result in dysfunction and burnout (see *Figure 1: The Human Function Curve*).

Now consider the effect of minimising your inner demands on your stress levels.

> Q: Estimate how much your stress levels could be reduced by lowering your internal demands (the process by which will be discussed shortly in C: Control).

External Demand

In the workplace, an example of external demand is workload, where increased workload can lead to increased stress.

Q: What are some external demands specific to
   your workplace?

Figure 3: External Stressors lists some of the common demands
faced in the workplace, such as workload, working hours,
cramped space, noise pollution, and unsafe conditions.

Sleep deprivation, for instance, is a major cause of stress. Anyone
working irregular hours and nightshift can testify to the feeling
of perpetual jetlag: anger is easily flared; concentration is poor;
muscles feel weak and tired.

In fact, it is widely recognised that shift workers have a higher
risk of illnesses, work-related accidents and injuries, and lower
life expectancy compared with the rest of the population.

It is also noteworthy that sleep deprivation is a well-known
instrument of torture, and that sleep deprivation causes death
faster than hunger.

External demand, however, is not just confined to the workplace.

Q: Which demands also apply to your home and
   personal space?

Now take a moment to consider what would happen to your
stress levels if you minimised some or all of the external demands
that are placed on you at home or at work.

Q: Estimate how much your stress levels could be
   reduced by lowering your external demands
   (the process by which will be discussed shortly
   in C: Control).

Snakes are a high trigger for stress. When we see a snake, our reptilian brain jumps into action and we feel the 'fight and flight' response course through our body with increasing heartrate, sweaty brow and hands, shallow breaths, and heightened vision. Fear, the midbrain response, magnifies the stress response.

But snake handlers have a technique that can override your 'fight and flight' stress reaction. It's called the 'Hiss Technique', and it's based on the sound snakes make—*Ssss*:

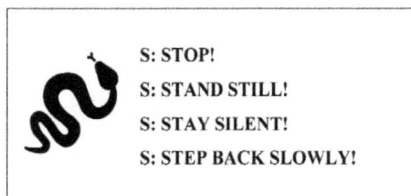

S: STOP!
S: STAND STILL!
S: STAY SILENT!
S: STEP BACK SLOWLY!

FIGURE 8: The Hiss Technique

When you are *aware* and conscious of your internal and external triggers for stress—when you see your 'snake' at work or at home—you can employ the Hiss Technique to minimise your stress (either in your mind, or actually physically enact the steps)—Stop! Stand Still! Stay Silent! Step Back Slowly!

You can be a snake charmer and charm your stress!

B: BREATHING

After awareness, breathing is the second step in short-term stress management. Just as awareness negotiates the first barrier to stress-management—your reptilian brain and its survival instinct—so too does breathing.

Taking deep, controlled breaths when facing a stressful trigger has three modes of action: physiological, emotional, and psychological.

Physiologically, deep breathing has two effects:

1. Decreases sympathetic nervous system activity, which is responsible for arousing the body for physical activity (e.g. the 'fight and flight' response).

2. Activates the parasympathetic nervous system, which is responsible for the regulation of the relaxation response.

The main breathing apparatus of the body includes the nasopharynx (nose and mouth), larynx, trachea, lungs (bronchi, bronchioles, and alveoli). But it also involves the largest muscle in the body, your diaphragm.

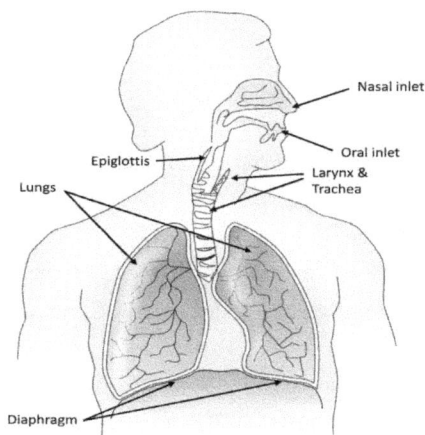

FIGURE 9:   The Human Breathing Apparatus

The diaphragm is largely controlled by the vagus nerve, which is part of the parasympathetic nervous system and down regulates blood pressure and heartrate. This is why with deep breathing you feel more relaxed and calmer and more emotionally in control, its second mode of action.

The third mode of action of deep breathing is psychological.

Your mind is usually not present. It is usually thinking of what's happened in the past, or what's going to happen in the future. Which is why it stresses.

But your body is always present because it's always 'here' and is therefore the gateway to being present in this moment of now.

For this reason, many mindfulness techniques focus on 'feeling' your body, such as deep breathing. The intention is to stop your mind wandering in the past and future and bring it into the present moment where it can de-stress.

C: CONTROL

After awareness and breathing, *control* the third step in short-term stress management.

Control negotiates the second barrier to stress-management—your paleomammalian brain and its emotional reactions.

Coping is another word for control. In the home and in the workplace, control equates to *the ability to determine demand.*

Usually our coping skills involve a mix of dealing with the cause of the stress—demand—and releasing or 'winding down' the stress that has already built up, like a pressure valve.

The effectiveness of coping mechanisms stems from your ability to re-direct your focus away from the pain of stress and onto something pleasurable, which is an example of what psychologists refer to as 'The Pleasure Principle'.

What works for some, however, doesn't work for another, but all coping techniques for stress share a commonality—we use them *to forget* what is causing us stress and in our deliberate forgetfulness our stress levels gradually diminish.

Control is internal and external, like the demands you face.

> Q: Using *Figure 3: External Stressors* as a guide, what helps you to control the top 3 external demands you face at home or at work?

> Q: How much success do you have in controlling these external demands?

Now think about internal stressors, the demands you place upon yourself.

> Q: Using *Figure 4: Internal Stressors* as a guide, what helps you to control the top 3 internal demands you face at home or at work?

> Q: How much success do you have in controlling these internal demands?

You have probably noticed that you expend a lot less energy in controlling your inner demands than external ones, as well as achieving greater stress relief. This is because it is far easier to control yourself than it is to control other people or situations.

There is a quick technique to keep in mind when dealing with short-term stressful situations. I call it the 'STRESS Technique', which is an acronym for:

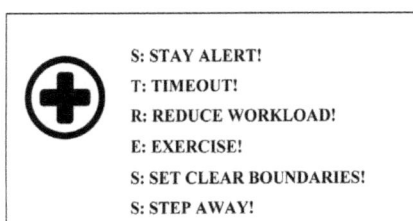

S: STAY ALERT!
T: TIMEOUT!
R: REDUCE WORKLOAD!
E: EXERCISE!
S: SET CLEAR BOUNDARIES!
S: STEP AWAY!

FIGURE 10:   The STRESS Technique

Stay Alert!

You have worked hard to become aware of your stress triggers and implemented deep breathing to control your stress, so it's important that your emotions remain calm and are not permitted to cloud your judgement.

Remain aware and keep breathing deeply to maintain your poise, composure, and peace of mind.

Timeout!

Sometimes taking time out from your usual environment can help to clear the mind of stress. Timeout options include:

- Talking with a friend or partner ('Chat time').
- Gardening.

- Retail therapy (as long as you only spend what you have saved).
- Yoga and meditation.
- Listening to calming music.
- A weekend break or mini holiday.

Reduce Workload!

It's often said that we overestimate what we can do in a day and underestimate what we can do in a lifetime.

If overestimating what you can do in your working day is causing unrealistic demands on your time and abilities, then reducing your workload will help to reduce your stress levels.

Good time management and realistic goal setting help to reduce workload pressures. This book does not cover goal setting, but in my book, *It's Up to You!*,[13] I discuss in detail how to set goals and manage your time.

Exercise!

Eating healthily and exercise are proven ways to reduce stress. During exercise, your brain releases natural endorphins, which are your body's equivalent of morphine and opium. Your endorphins have a natural soothing and calming effect on your brain and nervous system, which is nature's own way of helping you to reduce stress.

So exercise more to manage stress more.

[13] Scott Zarcinas, *It's Up to You! Why People Fail to Live the Life they Want and How to Change It.* DoctorZed Publishing, 2019.

Set Clear Boundaries!

A common cause of stress is other people, both at home and in the workplace. It's important, therefore, to set clear boundaries of what you deem acceptable in terms of other people's behaviour, demands, and attitudes.

Learning to say, "No!" more often can be an effective stress management technique.

Step Away!

Sometimes stepping away from a stressful trigger is the only option you have, especially if the situation is physically unsafe and potentially dangerous for yourself or others.

The physical act of stepping away removes you from the situation causing stress and allows you to regain control of your emotions and reassess your options.

If, for some reason, you are unable to physically remove yourself from the stressful trigger, you always have the option of breathing deeply and using this time to remain present and calm.

D: DECIDE

After awareness, breathing, and control, conscious *decision making* is the fourth step in short-term stress management.

However, when under pressure, decision making is often emotional or instinctive and unconscious, which is why we make such poor decisions when stressed.

The first three steps of the ABCD model annul the influence of your instinctive and emotional reactions so that you are in a position to make conscious and better decisions when stressed.

Conscious decision making negotiates the third barrier to stress-management—your neomammalian brain and its negative thoughts and beliefs.

Your ability to make conscious decisions has very powerful consequences because studies have shown that your choices significantly affect your happiness and wellbeing.

In fact, there's a scientific formula for happiness and wellbeing. Positive psychologists have discovered three key elements to happiness and put them into a formula:[14]

$$H = S + C + V$$

H: is your enduring level of happiness.

S: is your set range (genetic variable).

C: is your circumstances or conditions of your life (environmental variable).

V: represents actions under your voluntary control (psychological variable).

This isn't meant to be a mathematical formula, rather a guide to how you can improve your wellbeing. Not every element has equal influence over your happiness, however.

---

[14] Martin Seligman, *Authentic Happiness: Using the New Positive Psychology to Realize Your Potential for Lasting Fulfillment.* Atria Books, 2004.

For instance, 50% of your happiness is determined by your set range, 40% by your voluntary actions and choices, and only 10% by your circumstances or conditions in which you live.

This is why fame and fortune can't buy you happiness. Your circumstances can only ever make up 10% of your total emotional wellbeing.

Your set range is your biological comfort zone, the level to which you naturally gravitate. Some people are just genetically happier than others, which can't change much.

But it's your voluntary actions and choices that have the greatest impact on your overall state of being—including stress.

THE 4 D'S OF STRESS MANAGEMENT

Once you are at the point where you can circumnavigate your triune brain and make conscious decisions—not instinctive, emotional, and unconscious decisions—you have the power to affect your overall state of being.

You can reduce stress levels. You can increase happiness. You can make more informed decisions and make better judgements.

Figure 11: The 4 D's of Stress Management highlights the four quadrants within which you can prioritise demands at work and at home, and thereby manage stress levels.

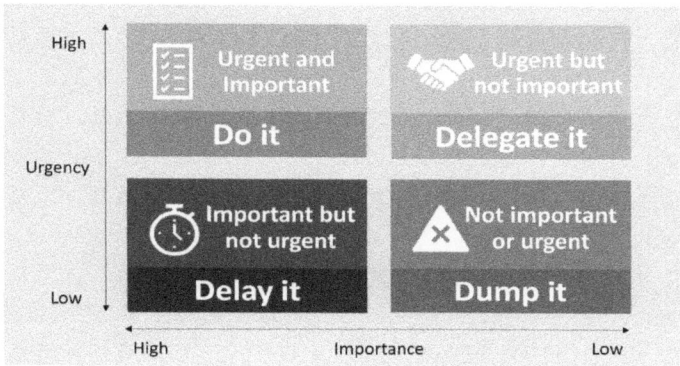

FIGURE 11:   The 4 D's of Stress Management

The manner in which you prioritise demands to reduce stress works like this:

- If a demand is of high urgency and high importance, you DO IT.

- If a demand is of high urgency but low importance, you DELEGAT IT.

- If a demand is of high importance but low urgency, you DELAY IT.

- If a demand is of low importance and low urgency, you DUMP IT.

MAIN POINTS:

1. The ABCD model is a technique for short-term stress management.
2. Awareness: be aware of your external and internal demands that cause stress.
3. Breathing: has three modes of action—physiological, emotional, and psychological.
4. Control: is the ability to determine demand.
5. Decide: your choices significantly affect your happiness and wellbeing.
6. The Happiness Formula: $H = S + C + V$
7. The 4 D's: Do It, Delegate It, Delay It, Dump It.

PART 2

FACING YOUR
FEARS

4 WHAT DO YOU HAVE TO FEAR?

'He who has overcome his fears will truly be free.'

Aristotle

IT'S BEEN SAID that the only thing you have to fear is fear itself.[15]

Fear is a survival mechanism built into the circuitry of your brain. Some level of fear is required to remain safe and alive, but for many, fear can be debilitating.

Fear is part of the 'fight and flight' response, but it can also cause you to *freeze* like a deer caught in the headlights of an approaching car. Fear can paralyse you. It can prevent you from doing what you need to do to get things done.

Whatever fear is stopping you, only you have the power to overcome it. It's your fear. No-one else can do it for you.

Living without fear, however, doesn't meant that fear isn't present. It just means that you no longer let it control who you are and what you do.

Fear will always arise. There will never be a time when it isn't lurking in the back of your mind. But will it stop you from doing what you have to do? Will it stop you from doing what's right?

Will it stop you from living your dream?

---

[15] Franklin D. Roosevelt, first inaugural address, 1932.

Your fears can become a habit like any other habit. But, just like background noise, years of fearful thoughts and worries can desensitise your mind to such an extent that you probably don't even know it's there.

But fear is a habit you must break if you are serious about minimizing stress and improving your wellbeing. When you break through your fears, you empower yourself.

And when you are empowered, you can begin to live a life that's true to you—one that's productive, prosperous, and purposeful.

FEAR IS HUMAN

There isn't a person alive who hasn't experienced fear of some description. Even those who appear fearless experience fear; they've just learned how to limit its control over them.

They also know a little secret:

Your success lies on the other side of your fear.

Which is why they are generally successful—they want success more than comfort. They are prepared to step outside their comfort zone, and that invariably means taking risks and stepping through their fears.

Yet this may be a bridge too far. A workplace and office survey conducted in the USA and Europe[16] revealed that 84% of employees harbour at least one type of irrational fear, and that 66% won't do something if they think it's going to be too hard.

[16] Vanson Bourne, Office Survey, 2013, commissioned by Mozy.com.

They also found that 23% of employees constantly worry that they are going to get the sack, that 1 in 5 are horrified of snakes and spiders, and that one quarter fear sending an email to the wrong person.

Significantly, this survey also put a price on workplace fears. They estimated that an incredible 189% of ROI is required to overcome perceived technology risk. Not only does fear have a negative effect on staff, it also effects the bottom line of business.

There is probably a big discrepancy between what your fear levels currently are and what you would like them to be. Remember, though, like stress there is a minimal requirement of fear, if only to act as a survival mechanism in immediately life-threatening situations. Too much fear, however, is dysfunctional and can lead to anxiety disorders and phobias.

The technique of *Facing Your Fears* described in Chapter 6 is designed to help you achieve an 80-90% reduction in your current fear levels and keep them at that 'survival zone' level.

Let's now discuss the different types of fears you might experience.

TYPES OF FEAR

There are just as many fears as there are people on the planet. That's because each fear is deeply personal and effects each person in a unique and individual way.

Q: What are some words you associate with 'fear'?

What is fearful to some, is a walk in the park for others. What causes fear in one will not cause fear in another. Fear is a learned response to a situation or event (see *The 3 Natural Fears* in the next chapter) that is a highly subjective and personalised experience.

Yet, there are a broad range of fears that are commonly experienced by many. The fear of old age is one. The fear of infirmary is another. So too the fear of flying.

> Q: What are some types of fears you are familiar
> with or have even experienced?

Below is a list of common fears:

- Public speaking
- Death
- Illness
- Poverty
- Flying
- Open or closed spaces
- Crowds
- Rejection, disapproval
- Water
- Needles
- Strangers
- Blood
- Animals (e.g. sharks, dogs)
- Insects (e.g. bees, spiders)
- Success and/or failure
- Darkness
- Lightning
- Germs
- Clowns
- Commitment/marriage
- Tornados, hurricanes
- Heights

Fears often fall into 1 of 3 categories:[17]

[17] The DSM-IV of the American Psychiatric Association lists 3 types of phobias, which are a disorder of fear, as :Agoraphobia, Social phobia, and Specific phobia.

Escape: the fear of being in *places* from which escape might be difficult or embarrassing, such as the fear of crowds.

Exposure: the fear of exposure elicited by certain types of *social or performance* situations, such as public speaking.

Exclusive: the fear of being in the presence of a *specific stimulus*, which commonly elicits avoidance of that stimulus, such as the fear of dogs.

Of the exclusive or specific types of fears, there are 4 main sub-types:

1. Animal fears: e.g. horses, sharks, spiders.
2. Environmental fears: e.g. hurricanes, water, lightning.
3. Situational fears: e.g. elevators, flying, bridges.
4. Injury fears: e.g. needles, blood, medical procedures.

FIGURE 12:   Types of Fear

Identifying and naming your fears is a powerful first step to reduce the impact of fear on your wellbeing and state of mind (we will discuss this further in the next chapter).

Dr. Susan Jeffers was an American psychologist and author of self-help literature who wrote the bestselling book, *Feel the Fear... And Do It Anyway*. She said:

> *All you have to do to lessen your fear is to gain more trust in your ability to handle whatever comes your way.*[18]

Part of gaining more trust in your ability to handle whatever comes your way is identifying how you react and respond to the stimuli that elicit fear. Knowing what fear is and how it is triggered is a necessary step in diminishing your fear.

We therefore need to define fear and understand its effects on our body and mind.

Main Points:

1. Fear causes fight, flight, and freeze.
2. Fear is a habit you must break to reduce stress.
3. Your success lies on the other side of your fear.
4. The 3 categories of fear: Escape, Exposure, Exclusive.
5. Identifying and naming your fears is a powerful first step to reduce the impact of fear.

---

[18] Dr. Susan Jeffers, *Feel the Fear... And Do It Anyway: Dynamic techniques for turning Fear, Indecision and Anger into Power, Action and Love*, Fawcett Columbine, 1988

5 WHAT IS FEAR?

'It is not death that a man should fear, but he should fear never beginning to live.'

Marcus Aurelius

FEAR IS DEFINED by the Webster dictionary as a noun and a verb, as something we experience and something we do.

---

noun

1 a: an unpleasant often strong emotion caused by anticipation or awareness of danger

  b (1): an instance of this emotion

    (2): a state marked by this emotion

2: anxious concern: SOLICITUDE

3: profound reverence and awe especially toward God

4: reason for alarm: DANGER

verb

transitive verb

1: to be afraid of: expect with alarm (*fear* the worst)

2: to have a reverential awe of God (*fear* of God)

intransitive verb

  : to be afraid or apprehensive (*feared* for their lives)

The main symptoms of fear include increased heartrate, breathlessness, tremors, sweating, dizziness, disorientation, preoccupation with the feared object, feeling time pressured, the need to urinate, and the sense of impending doom.

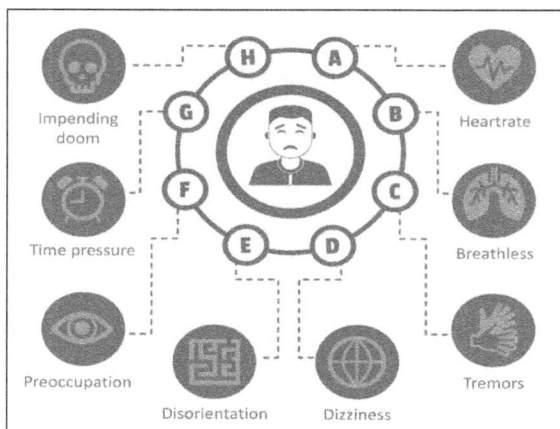

FIGURE 13: Fear Symptoms

You will notice that fear and stress share some of the same physical and mental symptoms, such as pounding heart, time pressure, and sweatiness.

This is because fear and stress are cognitive (i.e. thought based), which triggers physical responses in the emotional centre of the brain, the amygdala, which in turn elicits a sympathetic nerve response that we feel as physical symptoms.

Fear and stress are like two sides of a coin. Both are linked—fear can cause stress, and stress can lead to fear.

DISORDERS OF FEAR

Like stress, too much fear over a prolonged period of time can lead to dysfunction and mental illness.

There are 6 common medical disorders of fear recognised: Phobias, Social Phobias, Separation Anxiety, Generalised Anxiety Disorder, Post Traumatic Stress Disorder (PTSD), and Obsessive Compulsive Disorder (OCD).[19]

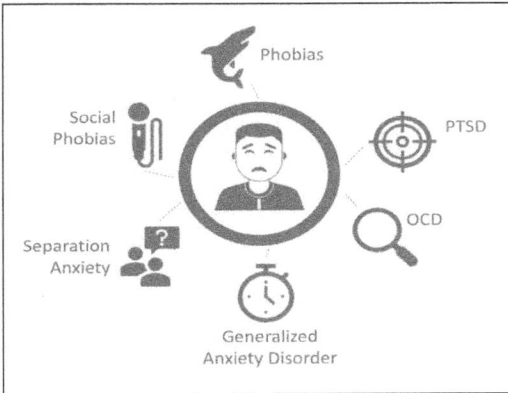

FIGURE 14:   Medical Disorders of Fear

Phobias

Phobias are irrational fears that interfere with a person's daily life or routine, such as work, sleep, or travel. For instance, if you have a fear of death and you plan your trips to avoid passing cemeteries, then this fear has become irrational.

Social Phobias

Social phobias are irrational fears of social encounters, which normally result in avoidance behaviour. For instance, if you have a fear of embarrassment and it causes you to avoid medical treatment for fear of being examined by a doctor or nurse, then this fear has become irrational.

[19] DSM-IV, American Psychiatric Association.

Separation Anxiety

Separation anxiety is the fear of being alone, abandoned, or separated from a particular person and even a pet or item of emotional or sentimental value. Children and adults can suffer from separation anxiety. For instance, if you have a fear of something terrible happening to your partner or child and you experience physical symptoms such as nausea, panic, or headaches when they leave for work or school, then this fear has become irrational.

Generalised Anxiety Disorder

Generalised anxiety disorder is excessive anxiety of no apparent reason or cause that lasts for more than 6 months. For instance, if you feel nervous, tense or fearful for no obvious reason and experience physical symptoms, such as restlessness, pounding heart, sweating, shaking, insomnia, or dizziness, then this might indicate an undiagnosed irrational fear expressing as anxiety, which may require medical intervention.

PTSD

PTSD is a disorder of fear that can happen after experiencing a traumatic or dangerous event, such as war, crime, accidents, abuse, and death of a loved one, usually within 3 months. As well as exhibiting the signs and symptoms of generalised anxiety, people with PTSD also have 're-experiencing' symptoms, such as flashbacks (reliving the trauma over and over), bad dreams, and frightening thoughts. They may also be easily startled, have wide swings of mood, and exhibit avoidance behaviour.

OCD

OCD is a mental health disorder characterised by thoughts that are intrusive, distressing, and obsessive, and physical or mental acts that are repetitive and compulsive. OCD presents in several ways, such as over checking (often for hours), contamination (and the need to constantly wash and be clean), hoarding, rumination, intrusive thoughts, and orderliness.

According to the DSM-IV of the American Psychiatric Association, 15-20% of the population experience a phobia at least once in their life, of which 95% begin before the age of 20 years. Women, too, are almost twice as likely to suffer from a phobia than men.

The National Institute of Mental Health, USA, recognise phobias as the most common mental disorder in the USA, and that 17% of social phobias develop into clinically diagnosed depression.

Research from the National Centre for PTSD, USA, has shown that 7-8% of the population will suffer from PTSD at some point in their life. A World Health Organisation (WHO) report on mental health in 2001 indicated that OCD was the fourth most common mental illness after phobias, substance abuse, and major depression.

AUTHOR'S NOTE:

If you have signs or symptoms of a fear disorder, you are advised to seek medical help to investigate any underlying health problem that may exist.

YOUR 3 NATURAL FEARS

Although fear manifests in many ways, medical researchers tell us that we are only born with three fears:

1. the fear of *loud noises*
2. the fear of *falling*
3. the fear of *abandonment*

That's it. Three.

Which means that of all the fears impacting your life, all but three are learned.

In adults, these three natural fears usually transform into the fear of death, the fear of danger, and the fear of desertion, from which all other fears grow and flourish.

PERCEPTION FILTER	CHILD	ADULT
FEAR #1	Loud Noises	Death
FEAR #2	Falling	Danger
FEAR #3	Abandonment	Desertion

TABLE 1:   Your 3 Natural Fears

Take a moment to look at your biggest fears. The fear of poverty in old age? The fear of death? The fear of public speaking? The fear of making mistakes?

You have learned these fears. Your life experience has taught you to repeatedly express and use these fears to avoid pain. You have created a cognitive story, usually involving a bad ending, associated with an external stimulus, which arouses fear.

The good news is, because all but three fears are learned, they can be unlearned. You can change your story, especially the ending.

If you have a fear of needles, that fear can be unlearned. If you have a fear of enclosed spaces, that fear can be unlearned. If you have a fear of illness, that fear can be unlearned. If you have a fear of failure, that fear can be unlearned.

Brené Brown is a research professor at the University of Houston and bestselling author of *Daring Greatly*.[20] She is a pioneer in the field of fear, shame, and vulnerability, and asserts that vulnerability is not a weakness—it is the place where fear and courage meet. She says:

> *Courage is contagious. Every time we choose courage, we make everyone around us a little better and the world a little braver.*

> Q: Consider when you feel most vulnerable. Are there situations that recur often?

Recognising your triggers for fear and how that fear feels is extremely important in developing the skills to overcome your fears, which we will now discuss in greater detail.

---

[20] Brené Brown, *Daring Greatly: How the Courage to be Vulnerable Transforms the Way We Live, Love, Parent, and Lead,* Penguin, 2013.

Main Points:

1. Fear is both a noun and a verb.
2. Fear and stress share the same symptomatology.
3. Medical disorders of fear include phobias, generalised anxiety disorder, PTSD, and OCD.
4. Seek medical help if you experience any signs of a disorder of fear.
5. You are only born with 3 natural fears: falling, loud noises, and abandonment.
6. Vulnerability is not a weakness.

6 FACE YOUR FEARS

'To conquer fear is the beginning of wisdom.'
Bertrand Russell

THE PROBLEM WITH fear is that it acts as a magnifying glass—
it makes the feared situation or object bigger than it actually is.

It also makes you feel smaller and more vulnerable than you
actually are. It convinces you that you are helpless and powerless
to change the situation or how you feel about it.

Fear, though, only has power over you if you let it. Its power is
therefore its weakness because its power is determined by your
permission to allow it to affect how you behave, how you feel,
and how you think about yourself.

But *you are bigger than your fears* because you are the creator of
them. You therefore have the power to choose against fear and
to not allow it to dictate your life.

Because you have this power, you have the power to unlearn all
your fears and escape the stranglehold they have on you. The way
you do this is to FACE Your Fears:

F: FEEL It
A: ANTICIPATE Difficulties
C: CHANGE the Context
E: EXTRACT the Truth

#1 FEEL IT

Thoughts and feelings are mental energy that get converted to physical energy. What you think, in other words, has physical effects on the body. If you think stressful thoughts, your brain turns those thoughts into neurochemicals, such as adrenaline and cortisol, which act upon the cells of your body—your heart muscles contract faster, your sweat glands secrete sweat, your pupils dilate, and your breathing increases.

Fear and stress are therefore energy in motion—they are e-Motion.

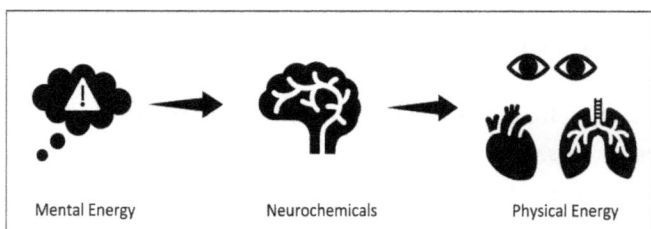

FIGURE 15: e-Motion

Because your emotions are energy, they are subject to the natural physical laws of the universe, such as Newton's Third Law of Thermodynamics, which states that 'for every action there is an equal and opposite reaction'.

This means that when you apply a force to something, an equal and opposite force pushes back against you. For instance, when you fire a gun the projectile force of the bullet is felt as a recoil towards you. The gun 'kicks back' when fired.

In emotional terms, this means that whatever you resist persists. If you fear a situation, the emotional energy you project towards that situation is recoiled back to you. The stronger you resist it, the stronger it 'pushes' back. This is the mechanism by which fear 'magnifies' the object or situation being feared.

> Q: What are some instances where a feared
> object or situation has persisted through your
> resistance to it?

Helen Keller suffered a devastating illness as a young child that left her blind, deaf, and without the ability to speak. Despite these disabilities, she managed to overcome tragedy and live a life of success and joy. Through her vulnerable physical condition, she learned that fear is a state of mind that can be conquered through non-resistance to it. She said:

Fear: the best way out is through.

You cannot pass through your fear and conquer it if you resist or run away from it. Which is why 'Feel It' is the first step in the process of Facing Your Fear, and there are 3 parts: Focus, Name & Tame, and Keep Focus.

1: Focus

When you focus on your fear you shine a light on it. Fear likes to work behind the scenes in the dark recesses of your mind, so when you shine a light on it you catch it in the middle of doing its mischief.

Like a thief, fear slinks into the shadows away from the light. It hates the attention.

Your attention is therefore a very powerful tool in defeating fear. Researchers estimate that the simple act of paying attention to your fear can reduce its impact by up to 40%.

Q: What is a fear you are currently experiencing?

Even if it is not immediately obvious, use the power of your attention to shine a light on it and then describe how it is making you feel. This exercise alone will have a significant effect on reducing the fear.

2: Name & Tame

The second thing to do to 'feel' your fear is to name it. Identifying and labelling it diminishes its power because something that is named is 'known', and what's known cannot do anything to you unless you allow it to.

A thief in the crowd is anonymous and can hide from your scrutiny. But once the thief has been spotted and identified, the thief will run away in shame. You've called it out.

Now you know its name, if it returns you simply have to let it know that you are aware of its presence. This is how you rob the robber of its power and tame your fear.

Once you have shone a light on your fear, put a name to it. Be creative; if you have a fear of snakes, you might call your fear 'Sydney'. If you have a fear of heights, you might call it 'Harry'. Some people even like to draw their fear in human form.

Naming or drawing your fear makes the fear less of a stranger to be avoided and resisted, and adding humour makes it less frightening and more palatable.

3: Keep Focus

The third thing to do in 'feeling' your fear is to keep focus: keep shining a light on it with your attention, and keep calling it out whenever it tries to sneak back in.

Be vigilant! Fear will always try to return, but if you keep the lights on and the alarm set it will soon give up. Fear will get the message sooner or later that it's not wanted. Like a guest that's unwelcome, its visits will become fewer and far between.

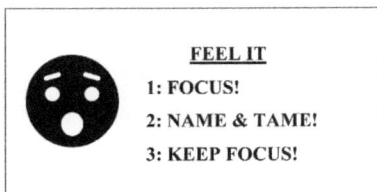

FEEL IT
1: FOCUS!
2: NAME & TAME!
3: KEEP FOCUS!

FIGURE 16:   Feel the Fear

#2 ANTICIPATE DIFFICULTIES

One of the habits of stress management is to write down your 'to-do' list daily so that you don't fret and worry about having to remember what you need to do.

This also includes bigger goals. In my book, *It's Up to You! Why Most People Fail to Live the Life they Want and How to Change It*, I mention that Brian Tracy, motivational speaker and author of *Eat that Frog!*,[21] says we should 'think on paper'. This is because writing down your goals employs both hemispheres of your brain, the creative right brain and the logical left brain.

---

[21] Brian Tracy, *Eat that Frog!*, Berrett-Koehler, 2001.

The corpus callosum is the central bundle of nerves that connects your two hemispheres. Without the corpus callosum, your left and right brain cannot communicate with each other.

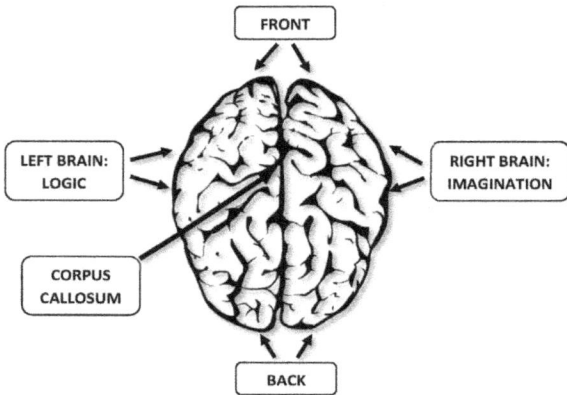

FIGURE 17:   Left & Right Brain

Setting goals utilises your creative imagination to envisage your future requirements (right brain) and uses your rational logic to work out the steps and strategies required to achieve it (left brain).

If you don't write down your goals and only keep them in your head, you are only utilising one half of your brain and thereby minimising your chances of success by at least 50%.

Writing your goals on paper, however, utilises your whole brain and maximises the chances of completing them. Research by psychologists at Dominican University, USA, in 2007 demonstrated that the act of writing goals enhances the achievement of those goals. Those who wrote down their goals accomplished significantly more than those who did not. The same study also showed positive benefits of accountability and commitment in the successful achievement of intended goals.[22]

The benefit of doing this is to help you anticipate any obstacles or barriers you are likely to encounter. You have clarity of the path ahead and can come up with a solution before the problem has even arrived.

This process also reduces the impact of fear. Because when you are able to anticipate some of the roadblocks ahead, your fears diminish. This is empowering.

> Q: What are some anticipated roadblocks that
>   might cause stress or fear for you in the future?

#3 CHANGE THE CONTEXT

Have you ever been in a situation where you weren't sure if you were scared or excited?

You might have been on a rollercoaster, or on a ride through the Haunted House at the fair. You might have even been watching a scary movie at the cinemas.

> Q: Name some situations where you have
>   experienced excitement in scary moments.

The reason we sometimes confuse the experience of fear and excitement is because the neurochemicals that are released during the 'fight and flight' response and some positive emotional states are the same.

[22] https://web.archive.org/web/20100610211058/http://www.dominican.edu/academics/ahss/psych/faculty/fulltime/gailmatthews/

But this is good news because the high state of arousal we experience during a fright can be transformed into a more positive experience.

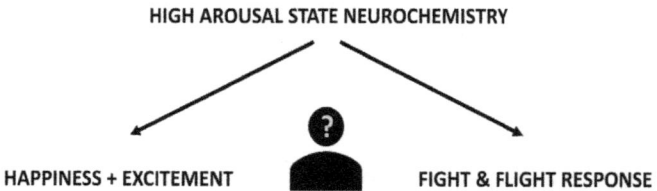

HIGH AROUSAL STATE NEUROCHEMISTRY

HAPPINESS + EXCITEMENT   **FIGHT & FLIGHT RESPONSE**

FIGURE 18:   High Arousal State Neurochemistry

Whenever elite athletes are interviewed just before a major event, such as the Olympic 100 metre sprint final, their answers are uncannily similar. If asked whether they are feeling nervous, they invariably answer, "No. I'm excited."

Where others would get nervous and go wobbly at the knees, elite athletes have trained their brains to interpret the enormity of the moment in a positive light. Likewise, you too can learn how to choose between a 'rush' and feeling completely terrorised.

The key is *context*. Research studies into PTSD suggest that context is a significant factor in how people experience fear—you need to perceive and feel that you are *safe*.

There are two main areas of the brain associated with the perception of danger, the hippocampus and the pre-frontal cortex. These higher-level centres of your brain (see *Figure 5: The Triune Brain*) process the situational context and evaluate the degree of danger.

If the threat to your safety is low, the hippocampus and pre-frontal cortex dampens your fear response. In essence, your higher brain centres reassure your emotional midbrain that you are safe, and when this happens you can change the experience of fear into enjoyment and excitement.

Think of a time when you took a trip to the zoo. When you saw the lions, tigers, and hippos, were you scared? Probably not, because these wild animals were behind walls or cages and you knew they couldn't eat you. You had the perception of being safe.

Now imagine being dropped in the middle of the African savanna with no weapons to defend yourself. Then you hear the roar of a lion close by. Are you scared? Of course you are, because your brain is telling you you're not in a safe place.

The difference between these two experiences is context. In one you feel safe, and in the other you don't. This is why you can switch from screaming to laughing on a rollercoaster ride or in the Haunted House.

> Q: Name some situations where you experienced a
>   sudden change of emotion from fright or fear
>   to excitement or enjoyment.

The commonality in these moments is the sense of being in control. This is not only important for management of fear, but it is also important for the management of stress (see *The Demand-Control Model* in Chapter 2), because when you feel you are in control:

- You experience residual gratification.
- You are reassured of your welfare.
- You gain belief in your ability to deal with fearful and stressful situations.

#4 EXTRACT THE TRUTH

There is usually a deeper truth to your fears that isn't always visible on the surface. Like the tip of an iceberg, your fears are the visible 10% floating above the waterline. The 90% below the surface is where the danger lies.

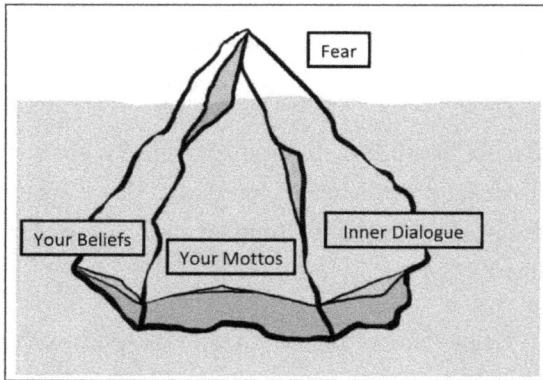

FIGURE 19: The Truth Beneath Your Fears

Your fears, therefore, can be used as a signal pointing you to a deeper underlying story that you tell yourself repeatedly through:

1. Your inner dialogue.
2. The mottos you say.

3.   The underlying beliefs you hold to be true
about yourself and the world.

1. Your Inner Dialogue

What is the story you tell yourself every day? What are the
things you keep telling yourself over and over again? Are they
mainly positive, or are they mainly negative?

Your story usually revolves around 4 common themes, which
you find in answer to:

1.   Who are you?

2.   What do you do?

3.   Why do you do it?

4.   How do you do it?

Q: When you answer these questions, does any
negativity come to mind? Do you use any
negative words to describe yourself?

Be aware of the words you use in your daily story, especially
the negative ones. Negativity can undermine your confidence,
and lack of confidence can diminish your feelings of being in
control, which in turn has a detrimental effect on your stress
levels and your reactions to fearful stimuli.

Now answer the above questions again. This time use positive
terms to describe yourself and note how this affects your
emotional state of being.

For instance, you could answer like Captain Kirk:

Q: Who are you? A: "I am a hero."

Q: What do you do? A: "I save humans (and aliens) from disaster."

Q: Why do you do it? A: "I make the universe a safer place to live."

Q: How do you do it? A: "I boldly go where no-one has gone before."

Okay, this is a bit of fun, but it's important to look at your life from what you consider to be an ideal situation. You don't have to describe yourself where you are at in this moment, you can describe who and where you want to be at some point in the future—then grow into that image of who you want to be!

Q: Who are you?

Q: What do you do?

Q: Why do you do it?

Q: How do you do it?

2. Your Mottos

Your mottos in life are an indication of the beliefs, attitudes and values you hold close to your heart. A lot of people don't realise they subscribe to a motto, but everyone has them.

Q: What are some mottos you like to say, or hear others say?

Mottos are taglines of your underlying belief system, and therefore your experience. Tell yourself one hundred times a day that all women are the same, and guess what your experience of women will be? Tell yourself thousands of times that life's a jungle, and guess what your experience of life will be?

Here are some common mottos that people stick to:

MOTTOS	
Life's a jungle; only the fittest survive.	Money doesn't grow on trees.
Do unto others before they do unto you.	The end justifies the means.
Money makes the world go 'round.	You need money to make money.
All men are the same.	It's a man's world.
All women are the same.	There's no such thing as miracles.

TABLE 2: Mottos

Your mottos and attitudes are important because your thoughts affect how you feel and how you act. Your thoughts impact your emotions and influence your behaviour.

Negative thought processes lead to negative emotions, self-limiting beliefs, and self-sabotaging behaviours. Positive thought processes lead to positive emotions, non-limiting beliefs, and self-empowering behaviours.

> Q: Consider the mottos you subscribe to, then ask yourself if they impact the way you feel (e.g. stress, fear, worry, anxiety), and if they also influence your behaviours.

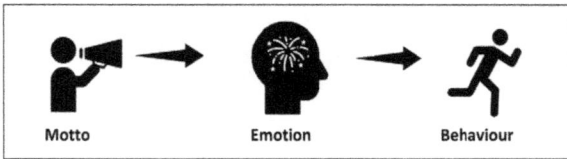

FIGURE 20: Motto, Emotion, Behaviour

For instance, the motto, 'Money doesn't grow on trees,' can arouse the fear of poverty, now or in old age, which can influence your attitudes and behaviour, such as money seeking and hoarding.

> Q: Now consider whether these mottos are actually true. If not, would changing them in a positive way help change your emotions and affect your behaviour in a positive way?

For instance, changing the above motto to, 'Money doesn't grow on trees, *but it does grow* with attention and good wealth management,' can create an abundance mindset and reduce the fear of poverty, thus influencing your behaviours in a more positive, enriching way, such as becoming more generous and giving.

3. *Your Beliefs*

Your core beliefs have a huge influence over your life. They are the guidelines you use to determine your thoughts, emotions, and actions.

They are a double-edged sword, however, because they can either empower you to success or disempower you through self-sabotage. For instance, where a pessimist sees a problem in every opportunity, an optimist sees an opportunity in every problem.

Your beliefs determine your perception of life and therefore your experience of life. If you fail to analyse your thoughts and beliefs you hold, you'll be destined to experience your past again and again until those thoughts and beliefs change. That's why it's been said:

> *You can't solve your problems with the same level of thinking that created them.*

There is a proportionate relationship between fear and self-belief—the more self-belief you have, the more your fears diminish. So use your fears to expose any false beliefs you have about yourself, such as 'I'm not good enough,' or, 'I'll never be a success.'

> Q: Try to identify any self-limiting beliefs that could be holding you back or affecting your ability to manage stress and fear.

For instance, the belief, 'I'm not good at anything,' can arouse the feeling of lack of confidence and fear of failure, which can lead to procrastination, avoidance behaviour, and refusal to accept responsibility for your actions.

> Q: Now consider whether these beliefs are actually true. If not, would changing them in a positive way help change your emotions and affect your behaviour in a positive way?

For instance, changing the above belief to, 'I'm not good at anything *yet, but I will get better* with practice and determination,' can grow your confidence and fill you with the joy of learning new things, which can remove the fear of taking risk and accepting responsibility.

WHAT DO YOU CHOOSE?

The time is now for you to make a choice: Do you want to continue living with fear, or do you want to live without fear?

You will need to be brave and have courage to FACE Your Fears, but you have the power to breakup with fear and neutralise its control over your life.

You have the power to do it. The question is whether you have the will and desire to.

As M. Scott Peck, psychiatrist and author of the bestselling self-help book, *The Road Less Travelled*, said:

> *Courage is not the absence of fear; it is the making of action in spite of fear.*[23]

---

[23] M. Scott Peck, *The Road Less Travelled,* Arrow Books, 1978.

Main Points:

1. You are bigger than your fears.
2. FACE Your Fears: Feel It, Anticipate Difficulties, Change the Context, Extract the Truth.
3. Feel It: Focus, Name and Tame, Keep Focus.
4. Anticipate Difficulties: 'Think on paper' and use 100% of your brain.
5. Change the Context: Positive emotions share the same neurochemistry as stress and fear; the difference is context.
6. Extract the Truth: Your fear is the visible tip of the underlying story you tell yourself through your inner dialogue, mottos, and beliefs.
7. You have the power to defeat your fears.

PART 3

THE WHEEL
OF CHANGE

7 WHAT'S STOPPING YOU?

'You may delay, but time will not, and lost time is never found again.'

Benjamin Franklin

IN THE INTRODUCTION I mentioned that technology has advanced more in the last 15 years than in the whole history of humanity. We now have the ability to access instant information at our fingertips, which brings great benefits but also a downside—a significant rise in stress.

It also has another downside—*procrastination*.

Not only has stress increased by 30% since over the past three decades, but so too has procrastination. In the 70s, the number of people defined as chronic procrastinators, or 'procs', was about 5%, or 1 in 20.

Today, that figure has increased 5-fold and is now 20-25%.[24] Which means that 1 in 4 people consistently and habitually delay tasks, either at home or in the workplace.

For a large part of my younger life I was a 'proc', one of the 20-25% who chronically procrastinated. For 15 years from high school to my late 20s, I told everyone I was going to write a book.

---

[24] Piers Steele, *The Nature of Procrastination: A Meta-Analytic and Theoretical Review of Quintessential Self-Regulatory Failure.* Psychological Bulletin, Vol. 133, No. 1, 65-94, 2007.

I had a love of reading, I had great stories to tell, and one day I was going to be just like my favourite authors and write a book.

But it didn't happen. When anybody asked me when I was going to start writing, I always had an excuse why I couldn't—too busy, too much study, too many parties, too little time.

But my favourite excuse was: "I don't have a computer." This was the mid-90s, when computers weren't household items. I could have bought one, but I didn't. I preferred to have an excuse why I couldn't write than a reason why I could.

I thought I was a doer, but I was only a 'gunna'. I was 'gunna' write a book one day. By now I was nearly 30 and successfully postponed my book for over half my life.

You see, as a chronic procrastinator, I had not yet learned this valuable lesson in life:

What you think about you become!

In other words, how you think is how you end up being. I eventually did write my first book, *The Golden Chalice*, and many others since then, including *Samantha Honeycomb* and *Your Natural State of Being*, but not until procrastination had stolen 15 years of writing away from me.

> Q: What are some of the things you have procrastinated doing?

> Q: What are some excuses you use to put off doing what you say you will do?

Here are some common excuses for procrastination:

PROCRASTINATION EXCUSES	
No time.	I was doing something else.
No money.	I forgot.
No opportunity.	Too overwhelming.
Too busy/too much to do.	I didn't know how to do it.
Too hard/I didn't feel like it.	It doesn't really matter/ It's not important.

TABLE 3: Procrastination Excuses

As the saying goes, "An ounce of action is worth a pound of theorising." Thinking is good, but it's action that makes things happen—action opens the door of opportunity.

But if stress is the 'silent killer', then procrastination is the killer of dreams. It steals your time, and if you're not careful there will be no time left to live the life you wanted to.

Figure 21: Productivity Curve shows how procrastination and stress are intricately linked:

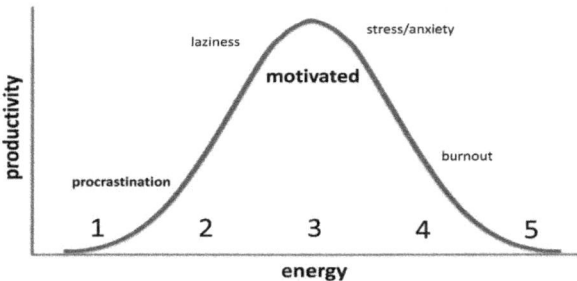

FIGURE 21: Productivity Curve

The horizontal line of the productivity curve indicates your energy levels. The vertical line indicates the productivity output in relation to the energy that you input.

The ideal situation is maximum output for minimum input, which is your 'motivated' zone. This is where we are at optimum performance.

Less than ideal is the 'lazy' and 'stress/anxiety' zones. When we're lazy, we input less than desired energy and our productivity level is affected.

When we're stressed, our productivity is also reduced to around the same levels as being lazy, but we're actually putting in twice as much energy as when we're being lazy.

The least productive zone is burnout and procrastination. With burnout, the more energy and effort you put in, the less productive you become. You are like a hamster on a wheel; you're doing a lot of work but not getting anywhere.

Procrastination achieves the same level of productivity as burnout, only you aren't putting in any effort. In fact, it's better to be lazy than to procrastinate!

THE 3 BARRIERS TO DEFEATING PROCRASTINATION

As with stress, your triune brain is a barrier you need to overcome to defeat procrastination.

The commonest causes of procrastination are:

1. Self-Limiting Beliefs (forebrain).
2. Pleasure and Pain Emotions (midbrain).
3. Safety and Survival Instincts (hindbrain).

Self-Limiting Beliefs—Forebrain

Self-limiting beliefs are those beliefs that cause you to lose confidence in your ability to adapt to circumstances, complete certain tasks, or achieve the result you want.

As Henry Ford, creator of the Ford motor company, said:

> *Whether you think you can, or think you can't, you're right.*

We will discuss self-limiting beliefs and the Failure-Cycle in further detail in Part 4, but suffice to say that how and what you think about determines your experience—if you think you can do something, you will; if you think you can't, you won't.

> Q: What are some instances where you said you can't do something and it has prevented you from even trying?

Pleasure and Pain Emotions—Midbrain

Your natural tendency to seek pleasure and avoid pain is also a significant cause of procrastination, which is known as 'avoidance' and 'arousal' procrastination.

Avoidance procrastination is when you do other tasks than the one that you know you should be doing. That is, you deliberately avoid the pain of emotional, intellectual, or physical hard work.

Instead of doing your tax return, you mow the lawns or do the grocery shopping. Instead of ringing that client and following up on their inquiry, you check your emails or have a chat with a fellow co-worker about this week's football game.

> Q: What are some instances where you avoided
>   doing what you knew you should do?

Arousal procrastination is when you distract yourself from what you should be doing. That is, you seek pleasurable or effortless activities over tiresome or boring tasks.

Instead of doing the ironing, you watch TV or play computer games. Instead of writing that business proposal, you check your Facebook feed or search the internet for cheap flights for your next holiday.

> Q: What are some instances where you distracted
>   yourself from doing what you should do?

Safety and Survival Instincts—Hindbrain

Your natural instinct for self-preservation is also a significant cause of procrastination, often felt as overwhelm and powerlessness, and is a trigger for the 'fight and flight' response.

When you feel overwhelmed by the task at hand, you go into 'shut down', which causes you to put off doing the task. That is, you don't know *what* to do and you procrastinate.

Q: What are some instances where you procrastinated because you were too overwhelmed to do what you should do?

Main Points:

1. Procrastination has increased 5-fold since the 70s.
2. What you think about you become.
3. It's better to be lazy than to procrastinate!
4. There are 3 barriers to defeating procrastination: Self-limiting beliefs, Pleasure and Pain emotions, Surival and Safety instincts.

8 THE ZONES OF MOTIVATION (1-2)

'In delay there lies no plenty.'

William Shakespeare

AS WITH STRESS management, you can circumnavigate your triune brain and make conscious decisions—not instinctive, emotional, and unconscious decisions—that empower you to achieve the things you want to achieve in life: health, wealth, love, and self-determination.

Instinctive, emotional, and unconscious decisions disempower you through increasing stress levels and procrastination.

Figure 22: The Zones of Motivation highlights the four zones within which you can focus on the causes of procrastination—self-limiting beliefs, pleasure and pain emotions, safety and survival instincts—and then devise an antidote to those causes to beat procrastination and start achieving.

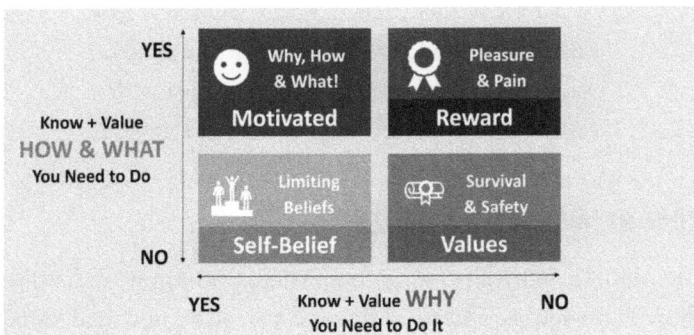

FIGURE 22: The Zones of Motivation

The vertical axis of the motivational matrix is 'Know + Value How & What You Need to Do'. This is either true (Yes) or not true (No) for you.

It's important to note that although you might know what you need to do, you might not value it—you might not think it's important or worth it. Or you might value what you need to do, but you don't know exactly what it is you should do.

To answer 'Yes' on this axis, you must be sure of both—you must know *and* value what you need to do.

> Q: What are some instances where you knew *how and what* needed to be done but you didn't think it important enough to do and it caused you to procrastinate or it caused you stress?

The horizontal axis is 'Know + Value Why You Need to Do It'. The reason or purpose for doing something must also be important to you and worthy of your efforts to do it, such as a cause you believe in.

> Q: What are some instances where you knew *why* something needed to be done but you didn't value the reason enough to do and it caused you to procrastinate or it caused you stress?

ZONE #1: MOTIVATED & DRIVEN

The desired motivational zone is where you know and value 'how and what' you need to do, and you also know and value 'why' you need to do it.

In this zone, all you need to do to keep motivated on the task at hand is to keep focus on the 'how, what, and why' of it.

When you are in Zone #1 you are in what positive psychologists call the 'Flow', the state of intense absorption where you forget yourself and your surroundings, especially when you are doing something creative.

When you are in the 'flow', even difficult tasks are accomplished with seeming ease. You feel a sense of timelessness and immersion with the task at hand, as if you and the thing you are doing are one.

> Q: What is an instance in which you felt in the
> 'flow'? What can you remember about your
> stress levels at this moment?

ZONE #2: REWARD & PRIORITIES

In Zone #2 you know and value 'how and what' you need to do, but you either do not know or you do not value 'why' you need to do it.

In this zone, you lack or have forgotten the purpose for doing what you need to do. The task at hand, even life, can seem pointless and meaningless.

Having minimal or no reason to do the task is energy sapping and de-motivating. Zone #2 is the zone of your midbrain, your emotional centre, the zone of pleasure and pain.

To move into Zone #1 and become motivated, you need to

accommodate the needs of your pleasure and pain centre through finding value and worth in what you are doing. The easiest way to do this is to reward yourself for your time and effort in completing the task.

> Q: When you reward yourself for the successful completion of a difficult task, what do you recall about your stress levels at that moment?

As a human being, you have certain physical, intellectual, emotional, and spiritual needs. These needs include being happy, feeling safe and secure, being appreciated and respected, having peace of mind, and being free to do the things you want to do.

If we don't feel our needs are being met, our triune brain reacts instinctively, emotionally, and with disbelief, triggering the stress response.

Unfortunately, this is true not only at home but at work, which is highlighted in a 2019 survey report that found up to 23% of employees felt their manager or organisation was 'horrible' at recognising them for their efforts and achievements.[25]

> Q: Have you felt you or your efforts went unrecognised at work? What do you remember about your stress levels at this moment?

Not only do we crave recognition and appreciation, people also want more freedom in their personal and professional life. A study by Global Workplace Analytics showed that 43% of

---

[25] *The Complacency Effect: Despite Disengagement, Employees Plan to Stay at Their Jobs.* Achievers, 2019.

employees who had flexible work time were more productive than those who had more rigid and set working hours.[26]

This means money isn't the main motivating factor for most people to work. The Glassdoor Employment Confidence Survey 2015 in the USA revealed that 79% of employees preferred new or additional benefits to a pay rise, such as improved parental leave. The same survey also showed that 37% of employees prioritise vacation time over increased salary.

What's more, according to *USA Today*, 58% of employees would agree to a pay cut in return for extra vacation time.

> Q: What would you value at work, that you don't
>   currently enjoy, more than an increase in
>   salary? If this were possible, how would this
>   effect your stress levels?

An African parable says that work will never end—there will always be something to do. You can't avoid it. Therefore, one of the best way to beat procrastination and work toward your maximum productivity is to ask yourself this question:

What are my highest value activities?

Your 'highest value activities' are the most rewarding activities where you get most bang for your buck. If you were to evaluate them using the 80:20 rule, these activities would be the 20% activities that deliver 80% productivity and the ones you should be focussing on.

---

[26] https://globalworkplaceanalytics.com/resources/costs-benefits

Lower value activities fall into the 80% of activities that only generate 20% of your productivity, and these you are allowed to procrastinate on, what Brian Tracy dubs 'positive procrastination'.

> Q: What are your Top 3 'high value activities'
> that generate 80% of your productivity? How
> would prioritising these activities effect your
> stress levels?

Identifying your 'high value activities' is the process of moving from Zone #2 into Zone #1 and becoming motivated.

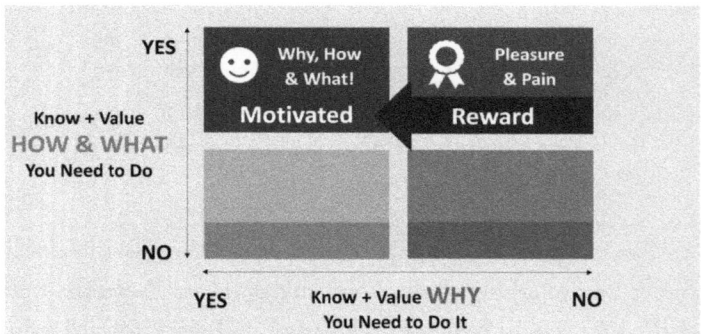

FIGURE 23:   Zone #2—Reward

THE RETAINED MODEL™

Everyone does something for a payoff. In our job, money is the obvious payoff, but there are other ways we get 'paid' for doing what we do.

Being valued and respected, being made to feel equal and welcomed, are also ways we get 'paid' from our place of employment.

In our relationships too, we expect to get paid with honesty, friendship, and loyalty.

But what happens when the payoff doesn't meet your expectations? What happens when the only reason you're in the job is because of the money? What happens when the stress of your job or relationship isn't worth it anymore?

There is a vast bank of research on why people leave their jobs and seek out new employment. Surprisingly, money comes about 4th or 5th on the list. Remuneration for our work is important, but it isn't the most important reason why we stay.

Other more important reasons include feeling entrusted, being included in decision-making, and having realistic promotional opportunities.

But the number one reason is, in fact, *appreciation*. We like to feel appreciated for the work we do and the person we are.

The sense of belonging is a natural human need. When we are valued and made to feel as though we are of worth and importance to our employer and family, we feel empowered.

When we don't feel valued or worthwhile, we feel disempowered and isolated—which is a recipe for stress and burnout.

In my book, *It's Up to You! Why Most People Fail to Live the Life they Want and How to Change It*, I introduce an exercise called the RETAINED Model™ to keep your goals aligned with your vision of who you want to be and what you want to do.

You can use this same model now to assess your priorities at work (and even at home) and keep them aligned with who you want to be and what you want to achieve. Consider this list of RETAINED criteria:

- R: Remuneration
- E: Education
- T: Trust
- A: Appreciation
- I: Influence
- N: New Opportunities
- E: Empowerment
- D: Direction

In the table below, now list in order of importance, from top to bottom, this list of RETAINED criteria.

		VALUE CRITERIA	YES	NO
VITAL	1.			
	2.			
	3.			
IMPORTANT	4.			
	5.			
	6.			
BONUS	7.			
	8.			

TABLE 4: Value Criteria

You will notice that the table is divided into 3 Vital, 3 Important, and 2 Bonus criteria.

For instance, you might list remuneration (e.g. income), new promotional opportunities, and education as Vital criteria.

Then you might have trust, appreciation, and personal empowerment (e.g. flexible work hours) as Important criteria.

Lastly, you might have direction and having influence in decision making as Bonus criteria.

You have now created a list of value prioritisation. Now consider whether these criteria are being met in your current job. Put a tick or a cross in the 'yes' or 'no' columns next to each criterion.

Now assign a numerical value of 4 to the Vital criteria, 2 to the Important criteria, and 1 to the Bonus criteria.

Add up how many ticks you have in the 'yes' column that correlate to your Vital criteria and give yourself a score out of 12. For instance, if you have 2 ticks in this field, then you score 8/12. No ticks equal 0/12.

Do the same with the number of ticks correlating to your Important criteria and score it out of 6. For instance, if you have 1 tick in this field, then you score 2/6.

Do the same with the number of ticks correlating to your Bonus values and score it out of 2. For instance, if you have 2 ticks in this field, then you score 2/2.

Finally, tally up your scores and give yourself a total out of 20. For instance, 1 vital tick, 3 important ticks, and 2 bonus ticks gives you a total score of $4 + 6 + 2 = 12/20$.

The score you achieve the first time you do this exercise represents your standardised score, the score that you compare to when you do this exercise again in the future.

There is no right or wrong with this exercise. It's simply a gauge as to where you see yourself in this moment.

If you scored 15/20 or more, that's fantastic. It probably means you're on the right path. All you need to work on is satisfying your Bonus criteria.

If you scored 11-14/20, you're probably comfortable with where you're at. But you would do well to sit down with your superiors and colleagues and work on how to satisfy your Vital and Important criteria, or even re-evaluate the level of importance of your criteria.

If you scored 10/20 and under, however, this could indicate a malalignment with who you are and what you do. It is an indication that your values and expectations are not being met. You owe it to yourself and your employer to sit down and discuss your current role, and whether there is scope for your Vital and Important criteria to be met in your current role, or even in another role.

The payoff for doing this exercise will be worth it.

Main Points:

1. The 4 Zones of Motivation are determined by knowing and valuing how and what you need to do, and why you need to do it.
2. Zone #1 is the Motivated & Driven zone.
3. Zone #2 is the zone of your midbrain, the zone of Pleasure & Pain.
4. To move from Zone #2 into Zone #1 you need to accommodate the needs of your emotional centre and 'reward' yourself through identifying your 'highest value activities'.
5. The RETAINED Model™ aligns your Vital, Important, and Bonus priorities.

9 THE ZONES OF MOTIVATION (3-4)

'Security is mostly a superstition. It does not exist in nature, nor do the children of men as a whole experience it. Avoiding danger is no safer in the long run than outright exposure... Life is a daring adventure or nothing at all.'

Helen Keller

ZONE #3: SELF-BELIEF

IN ZONE #3, you know and value 'why' you need to do something, but you either do not know or you do not value 'how or what' you need to do.

In this zone, you can lack the self-belief for doing what you need to do. You don't believe you have the necessary skills to perform the task at hand.

Having limited or minimal belief in your capabilities to perform a task is self-limiting and de-motivating. Zone #3 is the zone of your forebrain, your intelligence centre, the zone of thoughts, beliefs, and logical reasoning.

To move into Zone #1 and become motivated, you need to reroute your thinking around your old beliefs and thoughts through identifying and changing any limiting beliefs you have about yourself.

Q: What are some self-limiting beliefs that make
   you doubt your ability? What can you remember
   about your stress levels at these moments?

Your thoughts and beliefs are extremely important, because what you think about you become. If you think negative thoughts about yourself, you feel negative emotions, and you behave negatively. It is therefore vital to remember this:

*What stands between you and your true potential is
how you THINK!*

Researchers estimate that we have between 12,000 and 60,000 thoughts per day. Of those, 90-98% are repetition of what you thought the day before. Of those, 80% are negative, which equates to 3-17 million negative thoughts per year.

Imagine, though, if you had 3-17 million *positive* thoughts per year? Would this make a difference to your life and those you care for? What if I told you it's easier than you think?

Self-belief, then, is the process of moving from Zone #3 into Zone #1 and becoming motivated.

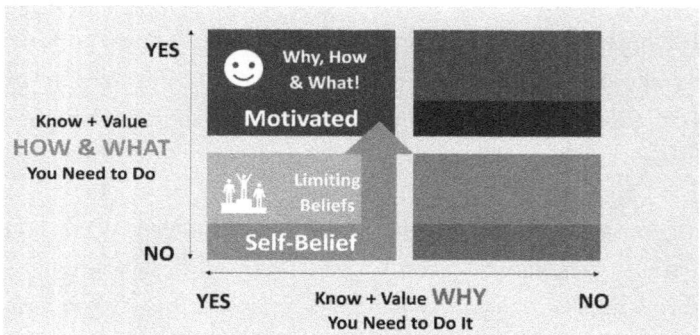

FIGURE 24:   Zone #3—Self-Belief

THE WHEEL OF CHANGE

Your mottos and beliefs are part of the bigger story you tell about yourself. Because it's a story, it can be rewritten, which requires a change in dialogue from self-limiting to self-empowering.

> Q: Have you changed an old, self-limiting belief
> you had about yourself and then managed to
> do something that you previously thought you
> were incapable of doing?

Changing a belief can be hard, but one of the best tools to change any self-limiting belief you have is *The Wheel of Change*.

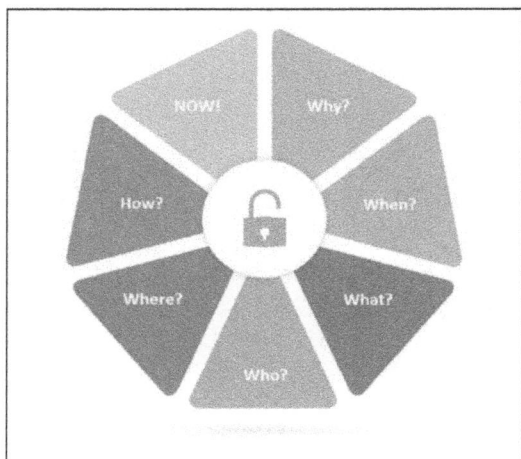

FIGURE 25:   The Wheel of Change

The Wheel of Change belief changing tool is a modification of multiple psychological and life-coaching tools available. I have created this tool to simplify the process of changing your self-limiting beliefs to those beliefs that are more empowering for you.

The power of *The Wheel of Change* is that it acts quickly by bypassing your main barriers to change: thoughts, emotions, and instincts.

Here is the 7-step process to change any self-limiting belief:

1. *Why* is this belief 100% true?
2. *When* has this belief not been true?
3. *What* effect does this belief have?
4. *Who* will you be in 5-7 years with this belief still in place?
5. *Where* will this belief take you in 5-7 years if it isn't changed?
6. *How* would your life change without that limiting belief?
7. *Now* is the time to change!

Let's now use this process to change a self-limiting belief that is causing you stress or preventing you from achieving your full potential.

> Q: Write this self-limiting belief on a piece of paper.

Now answer these questions from *The Wheel of Change*:

- *Why* is this belief 100% true?
- *When* has this belief not been true?

- *What* effect does this belief have?
- *Who* will you be in 5-7 years with this belief still in place?
- *Where* will this belief take you in 5-7 years if it isn't changed?
- *How* would your life change without that limiting belief?
- *Now* is the time to change—write down your new Self-Empowering Belief and commit yourself to re-reading this new belief 3x a day for the next 21 days. Note how this positively affects your stress levels and sense of wellbeing.

ZONE #4: HONOURING YOUR VALUES

In Zone #4, you do not know or value 'why' you need to do something, and you also do not know or value 'how or what' you need to do.

In this zone, you can feel overwhelmed and powerless to do what you need to do. You don't believe you have the necessary skills to perform the task at hand and you don't even feel the task has any meaning or purpose.

Zone #4 is the zone of your hindbrain, your instinctive zone of survival and safety, where fight and flight predominate.

To move into Zone #1 and become motivated, you therefore need to bypass your natural instincts. You do this by identifying higher principles by which you want to live and by honouring those values through your actions and behaviour.

Q: What is an instance in which your desire to
do the right thing outweighed your natural
instincts? What can you remember about your
stress levels at this moment?

Being true to what you value most in life, then, is the process of
moving from Zone #4 into Zone #1 and becoming motivated.

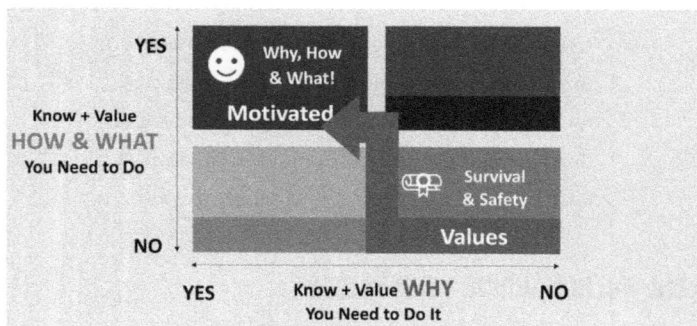

FIGURE 26:   Zone #4—Values

YOUR VALUES

When you value something you give it worth. This is true for
physical objects (e.g. a diamond ring, a car, a house) and people
(e.g. partners, family, friends). It's also true for ideas, beliefs, and
principles, such as beauty, generosity, kindness, and spirituality.

Your values are the standards to which you hold yourself
accountable, a collection of guiding principles that you deem
essential to live by, and they fall into 3 categories:

1.   Community values.

2.   Personal values.

3.   Core values.

Community Values

Community values are those values that you believe best suit the local and national community in which you live.

> Q: What are some community values that you
> consider important?

Some examples of community values include:

COMMUNITY VALUES	
Democracy	Diversity
Freedom of speech	Right to life
Religious freedom and tolerance	Abortion
Equality (sex, race, age, marriage)	Right to bear arms
Justice and liberty	Rule of law

TABLE 5:   Community Values

Personal Values

Personal values are those values that you believe best suit yourself. They are the ideals, the beliefs, the principles to which you hold as a standard to live up to.

> Q: What are some personal values that you
> consider important?

Some examples of personal values include:

PERSONAL VALUES	
Selflessness and courage	Purpose and meaning
Charity and gratitude	Leadership and teamwork
Fairness and forgiveness	Love and kindness
Religion and spirituality	Appreciation of beauty
Honesty and humility	Humour and hope
Wisdom and patience	Passion and creativity

TABLE 6:   Personal Values

Core Values

Core Values unite your community and personal values. If community values and personal values are two ends of a bow tie, then Core Values are the knot in the middle. Core Values are the reason behind the ideals, the why behind the beliefs.

Although there are thousands of community and personal values, there are only 3 Core Values. These are the common motivating forces of all people, the shared human needs we all experience. They are:

1. Goodness
2. Truth
3. Beauty

Since the time of Plato, Goodness, Truth and Beauty have been the three noble principles of humanity. There are no higher values than these. There are no more powerful values.

As Einstein once said: [27]

> *The ideals which have always shone before me and filled me with the joy of living are goodness, beauty, and truth.*

> Q: Which of the 3 Core Values do you resonate with and why?

The Value Circle

The Value Circle is designed to help you identify your value strengths and weaknesses. It is divided into 7 segments:

1. Family & Relationships.
2. Career & Work.
3. Money & Finances.
4. Health & Wellbeing.
5. Learning & Education.
6. Fun & Adventure.
7. Spirituality & Ethics.

Using *Figure 26: The Value Circle*, your task is to rate each segment on a scale of 0 – 10 (0 being the lowest and 10 the highest).

For instance, you might rate Family & Relationships as 9 or 10, but Money & Finances as 3. Do this for all segments and consider how each is being honoured in your life.

---

[27] Albert Einstein, *Einstein on Politics: His Private Thoughts and Public Stand on Nationalism, Zionism, War, Peace, and the Bomb*, Princeton University Press, 2013.

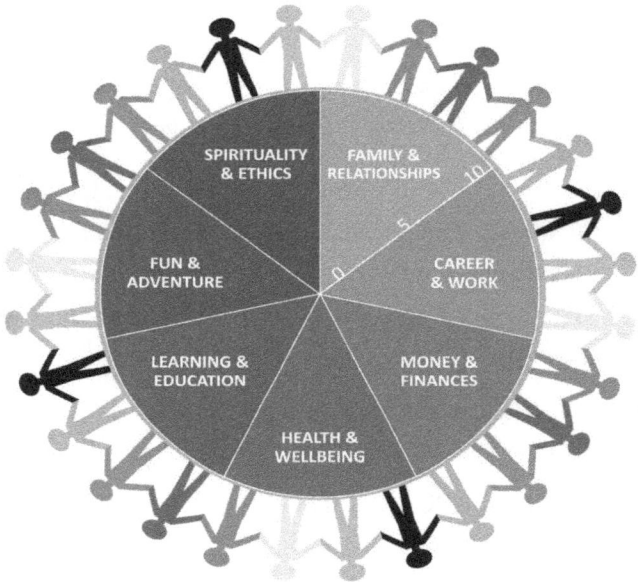

FIGURE 27: The Value Circle

Q: Does this reveal any insights that you were not previously aware?

The Value Pack

The Value Pack is a comprehensive list of values that you can use to identify your top 7 values. Directions for using the Value Pack (*Table 7* opposite) are:

-> Cross out or eliminate the values that you consider low or zero importance.

-> Circle or highlight the values that you consider *very high importance*.

FAMILY & RELATIONSHIPS	CAREER & WORK	MONEY & FINANCES	HEALTH & WELLBEING	LEARNING & EDUCATION	FUN & ADVENTURE	SPIRITUALITY & ETHICS
Belonging	Advancement	Autonomy	Meaning	Challenge	Adventure	Beauty
Patience	Competence	Financial Gain	Personal Expression	Knowledge	Change	Arts
Communication	Achievement	Location	Self-respect	Curiosity	Creativity	Democracy
Community	Fame	Power	Stability	Mastery	Leisure	Diversity
Cooperation	Prestige	Sophistication	Peace	Truth	Excitement	Religion
Love	Productivity	Security	Structure	Wisdom	Openness	Fairness
Loyalty	Teamwork	Status	Joy	Education	Variety	Honesty
Privacy	Reputation	Stability	Harmony	Collaboration	Nature	Quality
Recognition	Merit	Wealth	Humour	Innovation	Freedom	Spirituality
Friendship	Influence	Legacy	Wellbeing	Intellect	Fun	Goodness
Forgiveness	Balance	Philanthropy	Gratitude	Equality	Pleasure	Mercy

TABLE 7:   The Value Pack

-> If you have not circled or highlighted 7 very high important values, go through the list and add more values to total 7. These will not necessarily be very high important values, but they will be high important values.

-> Ensure that you have at least 1 value circled or highlighted in each column.

-> Now choose 1 very high or high important value from each column.

-> Rank these 7 important values from 1-7 (1 highest, 7 lowest).

Value Clarification

Now that you have listed your top 7 values, you can now write your values statement. Be as concise as you can in 3 sentences.

Here is a template to write your value statement:

1. My passion is [fill blank] and I believe my life purpose as a [fill blank] is to...

2. I value [state your top 3 values] and I dedicate myself to these values through [state action/ behaviours]...

3. I believe [state belief type value or meaning], which is best expressed through [state action/ behaviour/purpose]...

Feel free to use my value statement as an example:

My passion is writing, and I believe my life purpose as a messenger is to help others achieve their life purpose through coaching and mentorship. I value Goodness, Truth and Beauty and dedicate myself to these values through Giving, Forgiving, and Thanksgiving. I believe my natural state of being is joyous, acceptable, secure, peaceful, and free—and these are expressed best through living my being.

The more aligned you are with your values, the more happiness and wellbeing you experience. So ask yourself these questions at least weekly, if not daily:

1. Does my behaviour honour and demonstrate my values?

2. Am I true to my values?

3. Are there ways I can better align my thoughts, emotions, and behaviours with my values?

Main Points:

1. Zone #3 is the zone of your forebrain, the zone of thoughts, beliefs, and logical reasoning.
2. To move from Zone #3 into Zone #1 you need to reroute your thinking around your old beliefs and create new, self-empowering beliefs.
3. *The Wheel of Change* belief changing tool is the best tool to change self-limiting beliefs into self-empowering beliefs.
4. Zone #4 is the zone of your hindbrain, the zone of your safety and survival instinct.
5. To move from Zone 4 into Zone #1 you need to bypass your natural instincts by identifying your higher principles and values.

PART 4

THE BANANA TRAP

10 THE POWER TO CHOOSE

'Everything can be taken from a man but one thing: the last of the human freedoms—to choose one's attitude in any given set of circumstances, to choose one's own way.'
Victor Frankl

THERE IS A saying that knowledge is power. If this is true, then:

Inner knowledge of self is inner power.

This is especially important when it comes to de-stressing and controlling your emotional reactions and wellbeing.

Which is why mindfulness is so powerful, because when you are more present in the moment you are able to:

1. Increase your self-awareness.

2. Stay focussed for longer.

3. Make better and smarter decisions.

This means better results in all the important aspects of your life: health, wealth, relationships, and self-determination.

There are currently thousands of studies that show the benefits of mindfulness upon your physical body and state of mind, such as anxiety and depression, irritable bowel syndrome (IBS), chronic pain, addictions, and tinnitus.

Mindfulness techniques, such as meditation, also improve your health by boosting your body's immunity and ability to fight infection. It also has a positive impact on self-compassion, increasing your ability to be kind to yourself and less judgmental.

The table below highlights the main research findings of meditation and mindfulness on the brain.

PHYSICAL EFFECTS	SYMPTOMATIC BENEFIT
Increased cortical thickness and grey matter of the brain	Improved memory Emotional stability Heightened sensory perception Increased self-regulation
Reduction of Amygdala (Limbic System)	Less reactive, more responsive
Increased thickening of prefrontal cortex	Improved pain regulation Emotional regulation Better processing of distraction and conflict

TABLE 8: Meditation and Mindfulness Effects and Benefits

Jack Canfield, motivational speaker and bestselling author of *Chicken Soup for the Soul*, says mindfulness is so powerful because it grounds you in the present moment,[28] where you can focus on what is happening in the here and now and not on what has happened in the past or will happen in the future.

This allows you to deepen your awareness of what's happening in the current moment, as well as *how you are reacting* to it.

[28] Jack Canfield YouTube Channel, *5 Minutes of Mindfulness* series.

You become more aware of your thoughts and how they are *triggering certain emotions* and responses.

Then, once you are aware of your thoughts and their impact on you, it becomes easier to make better decisions and *easier to choose* better thoughts.

This is life changing because your thoughts are creating your reality, as Canfield says:

> *When you change your thinking, you literally change the way you experience the world.*

The real power to lower stress and improve your wellbeing is therefore not external but internal. The greatest results in de-stressing come from within—the power to choose, free will—irrespective of the control you may or may not be able to exert over your external demands.

Marcus Aurelius, Roman Emperor AD 160-181 said:

> *If you are distressed by anything external, the pain is not due to the thing itself, but to your estimate of it; and this you have the power to revoke at any moment.*

Your response to stressors, not the stress itself, is the determining factor in how you continue to experience the condition of stress. For here is the truth of de-stressing:

> *You might not have the power to control all the demands placed on you, but you can control the impact they have on your state of being.*

Therefore, the greatest impact you can ever have on de-stressing is your inner power to exert control and change.

THE BANANA TRAP

Jungle legend or not, The Banana Trap is still an ingenious method to catch chimpanzees. But our primate cousins aren't the only ones to fall victim to it. Probably every human being that has ever lived has, at least once in their life, become trapped in it.

That's because The Banana Trap is nothing less than *stress* itself.

> Q: Describe an event in which you have hung on
> to something that caused unnecessary stress.

The 'bananas' are the demands or internal and external stressors we hang on to, and they tend to fall into four categories:

1. Possessions and Things.
2. Emotions and Memory.
3. Pleasure and Pain.
4. Beliefs and Behaviours.

> Q: What are some 'bananas' that have trapped you
> in The Banana Trap of stress?

Each 'banana' is different and unique to each person because it is based on our thoughts, feelings, and personal preferences. What will trap some will not trap another.

Below is a list some common 'bananas' that trap us in The Banana Trap of stress:

POSSESSIONS/ THINGS	EMOTIONS/ MEMORY	PLEASURE/ PAIN	BELIEFS/ BEHAVIOURS
House & Car	Fear	Sex	Religion
Partners & Children	Anger	Sport	Atheism
Work & Career	Hatred	Entertainment	Socialism
Jewellery & Art	Pride	Drugs	Capitalism
Money & Power	Greed	Illness	Just Causes

TABLE 9: Common Bananas

Although it may seem daunting and overwhelming, freedom from The Banana Trap of chronic stress is possible.

This is because the one thing you have control over is *the power to choose.*

Focussing on your 'bananas'—Possession & Things, Emotions & Memory, Pleasure & Pain, Beliefs & Behaviours—and then choosing to let go of them, frees you from The Banana Trap and *keeps* you free.

THE PROCESS OF LETTING GO

Although release of pent-up stress is important and therapeutic, what is just as important is the prevention of it.

Preventing the build-up of stress means:

1. We don't have the problem of its recurrence; and

2. We don't have to find avenues of avoidance or unhealthy forms of release to cope with it.

It is far too difficult to control everything in our outer environment; there are just too many variables beyond our sphere of influence, variables which make a mockery of our attempts to control them.

That is why stress prevention is the healthiest, most efficient, most reliable, and in the end, most rewarding of all de-stressing techniques available.

But stress prevention has to be practical and reliable for it to be effective at maintaining low stress levels over long periods of time. This is where *The Process of Letting Go* can help.

The process is aimed at empowering you to live with greater joy, security, acceptance, peace, and freedom. It is a process of:

- *Awareness*
- *Responsibility*
- *Action*

AWARENESS

The Banana Trap has a high success rate. Everybody has fallen victim to it at some stage. Nobody is safe.

One of the main factors behind its success is unconsciousness:

1. We don't realise what we are doing; and
2. We don't realise the consequences of our actions.

> Q: Describe an instance when you only realised
> later that you were hanging onto the 'banana'
> and trapped yourself in a world of stress?

Think again about this instance.

> Q: Was the 'banana' that you hung on to a
> thought, an emotion, or personal preference?
> Describe it.

Fortunately, as with the design of the trap, therein lies the way out—and there is always a way out. The awareness we need to escape The Banana Trap is twofold:

1. The realisation of being trapped; and
2. The realisation of what we are holding on to.

For the first part, you know you have been trapped in The Banana Trap when you feel stressed. Stress is a red flag to your awareness and the message is loud and clear:

YOU ARE TRAPPED IN THE BANANA TRAP!

Once you are aware that you are trapped, you can question what is holding you in a cage of stress—the 'bananas' you won't let go of.

Knowing what you are holding onto is vital because it gives you a choice:

To keep holding and remain trapped, or to let go and be free?

Review the answer(s) you gave on the previous page.

> Q: How much stress could you have reduced, both in intensity and duration, if you were more aware of what was happening at the time?

RESPONSIBILITY

Responsibility is about self-empowerment. It's about taking the steps to greater autonomy and self-determination, which, at the end of the day, means choice.

It is up to you to take responsibility for the choices you have made and the consequences of those choices. It is up to you to understand the reason for the job you do, the partner you have, the car you drive, the alcohol and cigarettes you consume, the house you live in, the enemies you despise.

Then, once you understand the needs and desires behind all your emotions, thoughts and personal preferences, you are in a position to make a responsible choice—to remain stressed or to make a change?

The Blame Game

Another reason The Banana Trap is so successful is the lack of responsibility, especially for who you are and how you behave.

Football is cited as the most popular game on the planet, but it isn't. The 'Blame Game' is infinitely more popular and older.

Q: Describe an instance where you blamed another
for how you felt or behaved.

In contrast, some blame themselves for their problems.

Q: Describe an instance where you are likely
to blame, or have blamed, yourself for the
stress you feel.

Responsibility, on the other hand, is blameless: responsible people neither blame others nor blames them self for what is. Responsibility is an acknowledgement of the inherent human power to *choose* how to react and how to be.

Understanding Your Stress

Part of the process of responsibility is understanding the reason you have trapped yourself:

1. To understand how your stress levels got to the
    levels they are; and
2. To understand the role you played in the
    creation of your stress.

Responsibility is an exercise in getting to know the mechanisms of stress creation. Once you fully understand how stress is created, you can do something about limiting its effect on your state of being as well as its continuing production in the factory of your mind.

One of the most important steps of taking responsibility, therefore, is developing an understanding of the internal stressors—the 'bananas'—you are hanging on to. Then you can question why the 'banana' is so important.

Of all the 'bananas' that cause you stress through hanging on, focus now on the one that seems to cause you most stress of all.

> Q: Now ask: Do I really need this 'banana' I'm hanging on to? Explain your answer.

> Q: What do I hope to gain from holding on to this particular 'banana'?

> Q: Are the rewards for hanging on to the 'banana' real or false? Explain your answer.

Most of us know what we don't want, which is to live with constant high stress levels. But are we as aware about what we want to substitute in its place?

The choice to keep things as they are involves doing nothing save maintaining your grip on the 'banana' and continuing to live with high levels of stress.

The choice to change is a much harder choice because it involves action, and action requires bravery, to move forward in spite of fear.

ACTION

Once you understand your attraction to The Banana Trap, you go a long way to minimising its hold on you and closer to letting go of your grip on the 'banana' of stress.

For some, being aware and responsible is often enough to escape the continuing cycle of stress in which they have found them self.

However, if the original need or desire that initially lured you to the 'banana' has not been sufficiently dealt with, it will only be a matter of time before the desire resurfaces with renewed enthusiasm and you start looking for another 'banana' to satisfy its needs.

What's required is prevention or a long-term coping mechanism to minimise your stress levels and *keep* them at that level.

That's where *The Attitudes of Abundant Living* come into play.

Main Points:

1. Inner knowledge of self is inner power.
2. Mindfulness has benefits for your health, wealth, relationships, and self-determination.
3. Your thoughts are creating your experience, and you have the power to change your thoughts and therefore the power to change your experience.
4. The real power to lower stress is internal.
5. The Banana Trap is stress itself.
6. The Process of Letting Go: Awareness, Responsibility, Action.
7. The Blame Game is the most popular game on the planet.

11 THE ATTITUDES OF ABUNDANT LIVING

'Abundance is the process of letting go; that which is empty can receive.'

Bryant H. McGill

The three major *Attitudes of Abundant Living* are the simplest tools you will find to let go of the 'banana' and remain free of The Banana Trap.

The *Attitudes of Abundant Living* work to lower and prevent stress in two ways:[29]

1. Minimising demand.
2. Increasing control.

Being human means that you will always have urges, and urges are nothing more than inner demands you place upon yourself—needs, desires, wants, and wishes.

The majority of urges stem from thoughts, emotions, and personal preferences, and they generally fall within the four categories of: Possessions & Things, Emotions & Memory, Pleasure and Pain, and Beliefs and Behaviours.

The *Attitudes of Abundant Living* diminish the urge to continue holding on to the 'banana' causing stress and eventually let

---

[29] See the Demand-Control Model in Chapter 2.

it go, thus minimising a major factor in stress production—demand.

The *Attitudes of Abundant Living* also empower you through increasing your *control*, in particular control over the urge to stick your hand back into the cage and grab the banana.

The three major *Attitudes of Abundant Living* are time-honoured and easy to remember:

THE ATTITUDES OF ABUNDANT LIVING:

#1: *Giving*
#2: *Forgiving*
#3: *Thanksgiving*

GIVING

The *Attitude of Giving* works on the principle of what comes around goes around. Because no individual is an island, and because each individual is interdependent on everyone else, what you give to another eventually comes back to you.

> Q: Describe an instance where you lowered your
> stress through giving rather than receiving.

Generosity rewards itself. The happiest people are those who have learned that it is far better to give than to receive, giving to others what they wish to engender in themselves.

Giving to others what we desire ourselves is the best means of receiving them. If you want joy, give others joy. If you want security, make others feel secure. If you want to be accepted, make others feel welcomed. If you want peace, radiate peace to others. If you want freedom, help to liberate others.

For here is a fundamental truth of life:

Whatever you wish for yourself, first give to another.

Remember, though, the intent of giving must be true in order to reap the full benefits of de-stressing. Giving with true intent is what I call 'Unconditional Generosity' and there are four criteria (RICE):

1.   R: Giving without *Recognition.*
2.   I: Giving without *Impatience.*
3.   C: Giving without *Condition.*
4.   E: Giving without *Expectation.*

Q: Describe an instance where you have given something expecting others to recognise your generosity and it *wasn't forthcoming.*

How were your stress levels affected?

Q: Describe an instance where you have given something expecting that gift to be used within a particular timeframe and it *wasn't.*

How were your stress levels affected?

Q: Describe an instance where you have given something with the condition that the gift was to be used in a particular manner and it *wasn't*.

How were your stress levels affected?

Q: Describe an instance where you have given something expecting to profit financially, personally or materially and it *didn't happen*.

How were your stress levels affected?

You have probably noticed that your stress levels increase when you give needing a return on your investment. This is because:

1. Recognition, impatience, conditions, and expectations are *increased demands* you have placed upon yourself.
2. Once in the hands of somebody else, you have *limited control* over how your gift is ultimately used.

Alas, people remain trapped in The Banana Trap because their attitude is not one of giving but of taking. Their attitude is not one of letting go but of possessing.

What you take from other people and situations will eventually be taken from you—leaving you stressed!

If you take happiness from others or other things, happiness will eventually be taken from your sense of being, leaving you saddened and cynical.

If you take peace from others or other things, peace will be taken from your sense of being, leaving you uneasy and anxious.

If you take freedom from others or other things, freedom will be taken from your sense of being, leaving you limited and constrained.

Unconditional Generosity, therefore, is a great means to let go of the 'banana' because:

1. You minimise your own inner *demands* through eliminating the need for recognition, your impatience, the conditionality of your gifts, and your expectations.

2. You have greatest *control* over your own thoughts, emotions, and personal preferences.

FORGIVING

Like gratitude, the *Attitude of Forgiving* is one of the best means of escaping The Banana Trap and remaining free of it.

Forgiving works on the *c'est la vie* principle of accepting what is as it is. Unconditional acceptance of what is—who, what, why, where, when, and how—means that you allow the present moment to be as it already is.

In contrast, non-forgiveness, or resistance, means rejecting the present moment for what it is, coupled with the need for it to change, usually immediately.

> Q: Describe an instance where refusal to accept things as they were affected your state of being.

Not accepting the present moment puts you at high risk of stress because:

1. Your own *inner demand* is that things should be different from what they are.

2. In reality, you have very *limited control* over external events and people.

Not accepting the present moment sentences us to being stuck in it, like the movie Groundhog Day, to continually relive over and over again whatever we are resisting.

Resistance, or non-forgiveness, is the 'banana' you must release to escape The Banana Trap.

To use another analogy, resistance to what is here and now is like a ship in port: until it draws anchor, it is stuck where it is—forgiveness draws your anchor and lets you sail free.

> Q: Describe an instance where acceptance or forgiveness of things as they were affected your state of being in a positive way.

Like responsibility, forgiveness empowers you through letting go of the 'banana' because:

1. You minimise your own *inner demand* that things should be different from what they are.

2. You have greatest *control* over your own thoughts, emotions, and personal preferences.

With forgiveness, you let go of the need for this moment to be something other than what is—to be somewhere else, to be doing something else, to be with someone else, to be at some other time, and so forth—which is to let go of the 'banana'.

This may mean forgiving whoever or whatever has evoked stress and pain in your life. It may also mean forgiving *yourself* for the things you've said or done in the past. And if you believe in God, it may also mean forgiving Him.

You are now about to be asked the hardest thing you have to do in this guidebook, but it will be one of the best things to help lower your stress levels and keep them low.

> Q: Write a list of people you feel you need to
> forgive in order to 'draw your anchor' from the
> past and sail on toward the future:

What, now, are you going to do about it?

THANKSGIVING

The *Attitude of Gratitude* is the third, but no less effective, of the three major *Attitudes of Abundant Living*. Thanksgiving works on the principle of fulfilment:

> *Happiness doesn't come from having everything you*
> *want... It comes from wanting everything you have.*

Gratitude for *everything* in your life helps you to want what you have. In contrast, ingratitude rejects what you have in favour of something else, which is a cause of stress.

> Q: Describe an instance where ingratitude affected
> your state of being.

Like non-forgiveness, ingratitude is a form of resistance to what is here and now: "I don't like this. I don't want it!"

Continual ingratitude for what you have puts you at high risk of stress because:

1. Your own *inner demand* is to want more of what you *don't* have.

2. In reality, you have very *limited control* or power to fulfil every single desire.

Ingratitude is an admission, conscious or unconscious, that life will only get better if certain criteria are met, or certain criteria are removed, which is an *internal demand*: "I'll only be happy when I get a job." Or: "I'll only feel more relaxed when I don't have to be here any longer."

Ungrateful people are not joyful or secure people. They do not feel a lot of worthiness, nor are they at peace with themselves. Ingratitude is the 'banana' they hang on to and the consequence—stress—visits them accordingly.

> Q: Write a list of things you feel you could be more grateful for.

Like giving and forgiving, gratitude empowers you through letting go of the 'banana' because:

1. You minimise your own *inner demand* for things other than what you have.

2. You have greatest *control* over your own thoughts, emotions, and personal preferences.

Happy people are generally grateful people. Stress is low and joy is high because they constantly give praise and thanksgiving for life itself.

> Q: How much would gratitude for the things you listed on the previous page increase your *want* for them?

> Q: How much would gratitude for the things you listed improve your *control* over your inner desires?

> Q: Lastly, how much would gratitude for the things you listed lower your stress levels?

Main Points:

1. The Attitudes of Abundant Living: Giving, Forgiving, and Thanksgiving.
2. The Attitudes of Abundant Living reduce stress by minimising demand and increasing control.
3. Whatever you wish for yourself, first give to another.
4. Forgiveness helps you to heal old wounds.
5. Gratitude for what you have reduces stress and increases happiness.

12 PERCEPTION & PERSPECTIVE

'Reality is a question of perspective.'

Salman Rushdie

People often quip, "I'll believe it when I see it."

But as we have learned through this book, your beliefs play a huge role in how you see the world around you. In reality, it's truer to say that, "You'll see it when you believe it."

The science backs this up. In today's high tech, fast-paced world, the human brain has reached sensory overload. In fact, the average person today is inundated with 5x the amount of information than the average person in 1986.

According to *The Telegraph*, the amount of information today is equivalent to 174 newspapers of 85-pages, compared with 40 newspapers worth of information in the 80s.[30]

Positive psychologists have calculated the amount of sensory information our 5 senses send to the brain, and it's an astonishing 11 million bits per second.[31] That equates to about 100,000 words per day being sent to the brain for processing.

Yet the brain is only capable of processing 50-120 bits per

---

[30] www.telegraph.co.uk/news/science/science-news/8316534

[31] www.britannica.com/science/information-theory/Physiology

second, so there's a lot of information that's getting compressed or filtered out. We're just not seeing everything that comes our way; we simply can't.

Putting it in perspective, it takes 60 bits per second of processing power to listen to another person during a conversation. If we add a third person, that means you have to use your full 120 bits per second of processing power to engage with two conversations at once. Which is why your brain goes into overload when another person enters the conversation.

In real terms, the limits of the brain's processing capacity means that the human working memory is only able to store 5 to 7 pieces of information at any one time (where these 'chunks' of information don't exceed 120 bits per second).[32] Some researchers have even said it's even lower, at only 4 pieces of information at any one time.

For this reason, the human brain has adapted to filter out unnecessary information. Researchers call this process the 'Attention Filter'. They even go so far as to say that the attention filter is the most essential mental resource for any cognisant organism.

This is because your attention filter determines which aspects of the external and internal environment you have to deal with at any particular moment. Most information is dealt with on an automatic or sub-conscious level, and the attention filter then lets through what it deems important for your conscious awareness to know.

[32] *The Magical Number 7, Plus or Minus Two: Some Limits on Our Capacity for Processing Information*, George Miller, 1956.

Millions of neurones collectively combine to create your attention filter, which constantly monitor your internal and external environment in the background of your conscious awareness to select the most important things for you to focus on.

Have you ever driven for a lengthy period of time and arrived at your destination with little recall of the outside scenery you passed along the way?

> Q: Describe an instance when you were doing
> something for a while but couldn't remember
> the details of what you were doing.

This is your attention filter at work. It has filtered out the external scenery and protected you from registering it because it isn't essential. Only when you are drawn to a particular landmark does it register in your mind, and therefore your working memory.

Your attention filter follows certain principles or rules as to which bits of information it will let through to your consciousness, and these rules are set up by your triune brain:

1. Your Beliefs.
2. Your Emotions.
3. Your Natural Instincts.

Your attention filter is why you see what you believe.

Reality, in other words, is a matter of how you look at things. Your view from the top of a mountain is different from your view from the bottom of the mountain. Furthermore, the mountain may look huge from your perspective, but from an astronaut's perspective in the International Space Station, the mountain looks like an anthill.

> Q: Describe an instance where you were able to
> view a situation from a different perspective
> and it changed how you felt about it.

LEVELS OF PERCEPTION

Your triune brain determines what you consciously perceive through the filters of beliefs, emotions and instincts, what we now know as the 'Attention Filter'.

There are two main ways in which this filtering process works, through negation or through affirmation.

The Process of Negation

The process of negation follows as such:

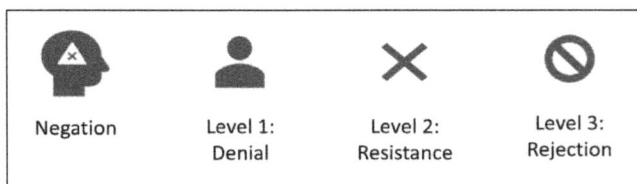

FIGURE 28:   The Process of Negation

The process of negation is not necessarily a negative process. In fact, it's an essential adaptation of the brain to sensory overload.

Without it, we would not be able to function in our day-to-day activities.

The first filter of negation is denial. This is the level of the reptilian hindbrain. If a stimulus isn't a threat to your safety and survival, your instinctive brain can deny it or deem it unimportant.

The second filter of negation is blockage or resistance. This is the level of the emotional midbrain. If the stimulus persists after the first filter of denial, your pleasure and pain centre blocks or resists the stimulus.

The third filter of negation is rejection. This is the level of the thinking forebrain. If the stimulus still persists after the initial filters of denial and resistance, your brain outright rejects the stimulus as being incompatible with its belief system.

An example of perception negation is the refusal to believe the earth is a planet in orbit around the sun. Flat earthers first deny that the earth is an orb. They also resist any evidence to the contrary, and lastly they outright reject the notion that the earth is anything but flat despite all the evidence suggesting otherwise.

> Q: Describe an instance where you believed a
> certain fact to be true or false but it later
> proved to be the opposite.

The Process of Affirmation

The process of affirmation follows as such:

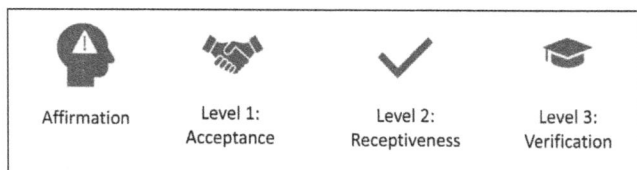

| Affirmation | Level 1: Acceptance | Level 2: Receptiveness | Level 3: Verification |

FIGURE 29:   The Process of Affirmation

The first filter of affirmation is acceptance, or agreeability. This is the level of the reptilian hindbrain. If a stimulus is considered useful to your survival, your instinctive brain can accept it as something beneficial.

The second filter of affirmation is receptiveness and openness. This is the level of the emotional midbrain. If the stimulus remains of interest after the first filter of acceptance, your pleasure and pain centre desires more of it and the stimulus becomes an item of attraction.

The third filter of affirmation is verification and knowledge. This is the level of the thinking forebrain. If the stimulus remains attractive after the initial two filters, your brain verifies the stimulus as being compatible with its belief system and it then becomes an item of knowledge.

This is the process in which all your knowledge is accumulated over your lifetime.

> Q: Describe an instance where you kept an open
>   mind about something, and it taught you a
>   valuable and unexpected lesson.

Breaking the cycle of stress is now a real and distinct possibility, both in the short term and the long term.

The final technique is what I call Attentive Action, and has two components:

1. Standing to Attention.
2. Taking Action.

STANDING TO ATTENTION

The first component of Attentive Action is 'Standing to Attention', like a soldier on parade. It has three essential parts to it:

1. WATCH Your Inner World.
2. LISTEN to Your Words.
3. OBSERVE Your Behaviours.

Watch Your Inner World

Watching your inner world involves being continually conscious of your thoughts, beliefs, mottos, and emotions. You must be mindful of how your thoughts trigger your emotions, particularly stress, and how your beliefs filter your perception of the world around you.

A good exercise to build your alertness is the 'What Were You Thinking?' exercise:

- Observe your current or present thought or emotion.

- What were you thinking before that thought/emotion? In other words, what thought lead to your current thought/emotion?
- Next, what preceded that thought/emotion?
- Then, what preceded that thought/emotion?

The aim is to trace back your thought chain as far as you can. A good beginning is 4 or 5, but with practice you might even be able to go back 10 preceding thoughts.

Listen to Your Words

The second part of Standing to Attention is listening to the words you speak. You must be attentive of how your words represent your thoughts and lead to your behaviours.

Take particular notice of the words that are self-limiting, excuse making, or disempowering:

- I Can't. I Won't. I Ain't.
- Shouldn't. Couldn't.
- I don't have...
- Why me?
- It's not my fault.
- I can't live without it.

Observe Your Behaviours

The third part of Standing to Attention is observing your behaviours.

Take particular notice of any behaviours that are self-limiting, reactive, or self-sabotaging.

The practice of detachment will assist you in observing your behaviour. This is the process of 'watching yourself from above', or as if you are 'out of your body'.

When you observe your behaviours in everyday activities, also take note of the motives behind those actions.

TAKING ACTION

The second component of Attentive Action is 'Taking Action', like a soldier marching. It too has three essential parts to it:

1. ACT in Spite of Fear.
2. FIGHT the Good Fight.
3. DELAY Gratification.

Act in Spite of Fear

In Chapter 6, FACE Your Fears, you learned how to minimise your fears through the actions of Feeling Your Fear, Anticipating Difficulties, Changing the Context, and Extracting the Truth.

This is how you take action in spite of your fear. You can be brave. You can be courageous.

Fight the Good Fight

Fighting the good fight is simply doing what's right in every situation. It's being chivalrous, like a knight in shining armour.

No matter what is happening around you, you have the power to always choose the right thing to do. No matter if everyone around you is behaving irrationally or irresponsibly, you have the power to choose the right course of action.

In the previous chapter, we discussed *The Attitudes of Abundant Living*. The easiest way to fight the good fight is to always keep in mind the attitudes of Giving, Forgiving, and Thanksgiving.

Delay Gratification

In Chapter 9, you learned how to honour your values in everything you do. When you honour your values, it's easy to put aside the need for instant gratification and allow time to manifest what it is you want.

Think of what dogs do: they bury their bone and wait for it to ripen before digging it up and enjoying it. They are the experts in Delaying Of Gratification—D.O.G!

Main Points:

1. Your Attention Filter employs your beliefs, emotions, and natural instincts to filter perception and allow what gets through to your consciousness.

2. The Process of Negation: Denial, Resistance, Rejection.

3. The Process of Affirmation: Acceptance, Receptiveness, Verification.

4. Standing to Attention: Watch your Inner World, Listen to Your Words, Observe Your Behaviours.

5. Take Action: Act in Spite of Fear, Fight the Good Fight, Delay Gratification.

HOW IT ALL WORKS

'Set peace of mind as your highest goal. Organize your life
around this goal.'

Brian Tracy

WE HAVE NOW come full circle. You now have all the tools and
techniques to beat stress and live with greater happiness and
wellbeing.

The practice of awareness, responsibility, and action brings
together all the necessary requirements for effective stress
management. As we have discussed throughout this book, the
cycle of stress begins with your triune brain—how you think,
feel, and react—which leads to self-limiting or self-sabotaging
behaviour. This in turn leads to non-achievement or failure,
which triggers a negative payoff and stress.

In Chapter 3, you were given the ABCD Model of short-
term stress management. With *Figure 30: Breaking the Cycle
of Stress*, you now have the ABCD Model of long-term stress
managment:

-> A: Attention! Watch, Listen, Observe.

-> B: Bravery! Act in Spite of Fear.

-> C: Chivalry! Fight the Good Fight.

-> D: Duty! Delay of Gratification.

The ABCD Model of long-term stress management breaks the
cycle at all four lead points in the Cycle of Stress.

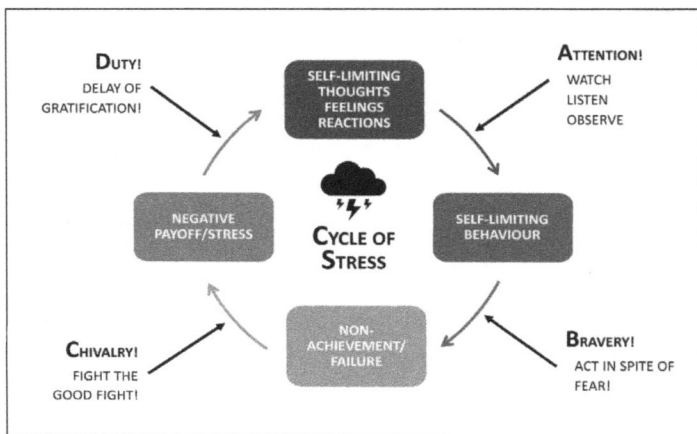

FIGURE 30: Breaking the Cycle of Stress

Attention! breaks the cycle of at the level of thought, feelings, and instinct before self-sabotaging behaviour starts through watching, listening, and observing your inner world.

Bravery! breaks the cycle at the level of of self-sabotaging behaviour by acting in spite of fear.

Chivalry! breaks the cycle at the level of non-achievement by fighting the good fight and implementing the *Attitudes of Abundant Living*.

Duty! breaks the cycle at the level of negative payoff through delaying gratification.

You now know all there is to know about destressing. You just need to put it into practice.

PUTTING IT INTO PRACTICE

To escape The Banana Trap and remain free of it is to be empowered. People who are empowered are people who have power over their state of being—the power to be who and what they are.

Empowered people are *aware* of:

1. What they think, say and do.
2. Their needs and desires.
3. The impact of thoughts, emotions and personal preferences on their state of being.
4. The internal and external demands that cause stress.
5. The necessary process to minimise and prevent harmful stress.

Empowered people take *responsibility* for:

1. Themselves and the environment in which they live.
2. Any internal and external demands placed upon them.
3. The stress they feel.
4. Being as much aware of what is going on inside them as what is going on outside them.
5. Any action required to limit demand and increase control of their inner and outer environments.
6. Their state of being.

Empowered people are *pro-active*:

1. Because they are aware, they know what appropriate action to take and what not to take.

2. Because they are responsible, they understand the impact of stress upon their state of being and understand the necessary process to minimise stress and prevent its recurrence.

3. Empowered people actively engage the *Attitudes of Abundant Living*.

THE POWER OF COMMITMENT

Remember back to the very beginning of this book when you assessed your current stress levels and your preferred stress levels?

> Q: How does it compare with your current stress levels now?

> Q: Now set a level of stress you believe you can realistically achieve following *The Process of Letting Go*.

This level can now be your 'stress' goal, but bear in mind that any success requires long-term commitment, and de-stressing is no different.

> *...until one is committed there is hesitancy, the chance to draw back, always ineffectiveness. Concerning all acts of initiative (and creation), there is one elementary truth, the ignorance of which kills countless ideas and splendid plans: that the moment one definitely commits oneself then providence moves*

too... All sorts of things occur to help one that would never otherwise have occurred. A whole stream of events issues from the decision, raising in one's favour all manner of unforeseen incidents and meetings and material assistance, which no man could have dreamt would have come his way.

W.H. Murray. The Scottish Himalayan Expedition, 1951

I now offer you a contract with yourself to commit to the principles of stress management outlined in this book:

CONTRACTUAL AGREEMENT:

On this date_____

I _____

do hereby commit to the principles of *Stress Management* in order to fulfil my goal of minimising my stress levels and maintaining them at levels in which I am able to function at my optimal ability.

I recognise that the power to control my stress levels is in my hands and nobody else. I recognise the importance of the process of letting go, and I recognise that the process of stress minimisation is a process that never ends.

I hereby make this lifelong commitment to myself.

Signed: _____

90-DAY CHALLENGE

Now that you've signed a contract with yourself to commit to the principles of de-stressing, I offer one last challenge to you.

After 90 days of putting into practice the techniques of de-stressing outlined in this book, you will notice a significant, long term reduction in your everyday stress levels.

If you feel that you have failed to achieve your 'stress' goals, after honestly applying the principles of short-term and long-term stress management, then please contact me and I will offer you free enrolment in any one of the Life Leadership workshops, seminars, or courses of your choice. Or you can choose a free copy of any of my available books from DoctorZed Publishing.

It can't be more stress-free than that!

If the content of this book contributes to your ability to better manage stress, I am delighted to have had some positive impact and I am grateful for the opportunity to help.

If you would like to learn more about my Life Leadership programs, I'd be honoured to help you further. I have devoted myself to making the world a better place by helping others fulfil their immense potential and to make themselves better people.

Dr. Scott Zarcinas

Connect with DoctorZed

Facebook: YNSOB.by.Dr.Scott.Zarcinas
LinkedIn: dr-scott-zarcinas-6572399
Instagram: doctorzed_motivational_speaker
Twitter: @DrScottZarcinas
Website: *scottzarcinas.com*

Growing great people is how you grow a great business!

Are you a leader of a team, involved in a team environment, a business owner, or entrepreneur looking to grow your business?

Ask me how I can help your business grow by growing your people.

E: scott.zarcinas@doctorzed.com
W: scottzarcinas.com/contact

The Life You Want, the Way You Want, How You Want!

Looking for a coach or mentor to help you get direction and take your life to the next level?

Ask me how I can help you maximise your capabilities and reach your fullest potential.

E: scott.zarcinas@doctorzed.com
W: scottzarcinas.com/contact

Book DoctorZed for Your Next Function!
Keynotes • MC • Presentations

scottzarcinas.com/book-doctorzed/

Other Titles by Scott Zarcinas

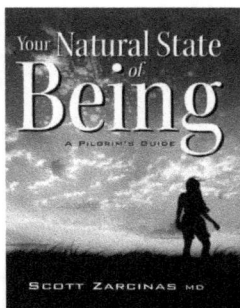

Your Natural State of Being
by Scott Zarcinas M.D.

ISBN: 978-0-6481315-8-8
eISBN: 978-0-9775969-4-2
DoctorZed Publishing

Available in print and ebook.

'Your Natural State of Being is refreshing. A tonic to read. Comprehensive and scholarly, it also has so many poetic qualities.' ~ Roger Rees, Emeritus Professor of Disability Studies and Research, Flinders University

You already have what you are looking for!

Ever wanted the answers to life's deepest questions: Who am I? Why do I do what I do? What am I doing with my life?

Your Natural State of Being helps you answer these questions by getting to the heart of the motivating forces and innermost needs of your life.

But unlike 'quick fix' and 'step-by-step' guides it offers real solutions through the understanding of your true self.

www.scottzarcinas.com/books/your-natural-state-of-being

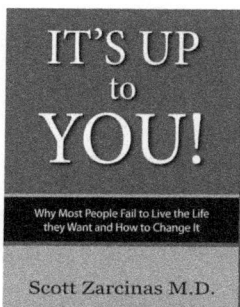

It's Up to You! Why Most People Fail to Live the Life they Want and How to Change It
by Scott Zarcinas M.D.
ISBN: 978-06485726-5-7
eISBN: 978-06485726-3-3
DoctorZed Publishing

Available in print and ebook.

Featuring 9 Life Leadership Strategies to Live the Life You Want, the Way You Want, How You Want.

Do you feel stuck in a rut? Is your life on hold? Are you looking for new direction but don't know which way to turn?

We all want to do more than just survive; we want to thrive. But if you're trapped in the same old routine, now is the time to start living the life you were born to live—with abundance.

This book is your go-to manual if:

• You need a break from the old and to take a new direction.

• You desire greater success and fulfillment.

• You seek the confidence to be yourself and not what others expect you to be.

www.scottzarcinas.com/books/its-up-to-you

www.ingramcontent.com/pod-product-compliance
Lightning Source LLC
Chambersburg PA
CBHW030934090426
42737CB00007B/429